张惠芬 ● 编著

张老师教汉字

汉字拼读课本 上

LEARNING
CHINESE CHARACTERS
FROM MS. ZHANG

FROM CHARACTERS TO WORDS (A)

英译 · 沈叙伦

北京语言大学出版社
BEIJING LANGUAGE AND CULTURE
UNIVERSITY PRESS

图书在版编目（CIP）数据

张老师教汉字·汉字拼读课本（上）/ 张惠芬编著.
—北京：北京语言大学出版社，2009 重印
ISBN 978 - 7 - 5619 - 1293 - 5

Ⅰ. 张…
Ⅱ. 张…
Ⅲ. 汉字 - 对外汉语教学 - 教材
Ⅳ. H195.4

中国版本图书馆 CIP 数据核字(2004)第 016434 号

书　　名：张老师教汉字·汉字拼读课本（上）
责任印制：陈　辉

出版发行：北京语言大学出版社
社　　址：北京市海淀区学院路 15 号　邮政编码：100083
网　　址：www.blcup.com
电　　话：发行部　82303650 / 3591 / 3651
　　　　　编辑部　82303647
　　　　　读者服务部　82303653 / 3908
　　　　　网上订购电话　82303668
　　　　　客户服务信箱　service@blcup.net
印　　刷：北京中科印刷有限公司
经　　销：全国新华书店

版　　次：2006 年 2 月第 1 版　2009 年 7 月第 3 次印刷
开　　本：787 毫米×1092 毫米　1/16　印张：14.5
字　　数：216 千字　　印数：5001 - 8000 册
书　　号：ISBN 978 - 7 - 5619 - 1293 - 5 / H·04015
定　　价：39.00 元

凡有印装质量问题，本社负责调换。电话：82303590

使 用 建 议

　　《张老师教汉字》是为零起点来华留学生、特别是非汉字文化圈的初学者编写的汉字选修课教材。本教材根据来华留学生汉字学习的实际情况,编为《汉字识写课本》和《汉字拼读课本》两种,使写字教学和识字教学适当分流。

　　(1)《汉字识写课本》用"图画法"作为形义联想的生发点,以形声字形旁归类为主线,侧重汉字的书写、字源分析和形体结构分析,旨在帮助学习者清晰构建与汉字相适应的认知结构。

　　(2)《汉字拼读课本》用"拼形法"建立汉字之间的关系联想和类推,以形声字声旁归类为主线,在"记忆窍门"的形式中凸显汉字学习策略,意在给学生一个系统,将构字规律转化为识字规律。

　　(3)为更有效地掌握汉字,本教材还注意字义与词义的关系,给所学汉字提供了一些由该字组成的词,又给每一个应当掌握的词提供了例句,希望在语境中加深对这些字、词的理解。

　　(4)本教材还在汉字教学的同时介绍汉字学习策略,体现再循环汉字记忆法,遇生想熟,寻找相似;以熟带生,扩展类化,在不断复现、推演中掌握尽可能多的汉字。

　　《张老师教汉字》依据国家汉办《汉字水平词汇与汉字等级大纲》,共收录汉字 1885 个,包括全部甲、乙级字以及 260 多个丙、丁级字,另外还有 20 个超纲字,如"翰""韩""酪"等,以补学生所需。《汉字识写课本》收录汉字 780 个,其中甲级字 630 个左右,乙级字 120 多个,以及少量的作为部首的丙、丁级字。

　　《汉字识写课本》共 25 课,《汉字拼读课本》共 30 课,每课均需两课时。

　　《汉字识写课本》配有练习册,《汉字拼读课本》配有 CD。

北京语言大学　　张惠芬
2005 年 6 月

Suggestions on How to Use

Learning Chinese Characters from Ms. Zhang is a set of textbooks for an elective course of Chinese characters for foreign students in China without any Chinese learning experience, especially those beginners coming from the non-Chinese character-culture. In consideration of the real situation, in which those foreign students learn Chinese characters in China, this set of textbooks includes *Reading and Writing Chinese Characters and From Characters to Words*, separating in a proper way the teaching of writing Chinese characters from that of reading Chinese characters.

1. With the help of pictures, *Reading and Writing Chinese Characters* encourages learners to associate pictographic elements with meanings. Grouping pictophonetic characters by their pictographic elements, the book lays special emphasis on writing characters and analyzing the origin and structure of the characters, aiming at helping learners establish a cognitive construct for Chinese characters.

2. Highlighting the formation of a character by combining different component parts, *From Characters to Words* establishes association and analogy among Chinese characters. The book groups pictophonetic characters by their phonetic elements and provides various tips for memorizing characters, aiming at helping learners master a system, by which they can change the regular pattern of Chinese characters' formation into a law of learning Chinese characters.

3. To help learners master Chinese characters effectively, the set of textbooks pays attention to the relationship between the meaning of the char-

acter and that of the word by offering some words formed by using the character being learned and providing some example sentences for each of the words to be mastered. It is hoped that learners will gain a better understanding of the characters and the words in context.

4. While carrying out Chinese characters teaching, the set of textbooks also introduces various learning strategies, such as memorizing characters by recycling them repeatedly, associating new characters with the familiar ones by finding the similarity between them, and learning new characters with the help of the old ones etc. These strategies will assist learners to master more Chinese characters.

In accordance with HSK Guidelines for Chinese Words and Characters issued by the National Office for Teaching Chinese as a Foreign Language, *Learning Characters from Ms. Zhang* includes 1, 885 Chinese characters altogether, among which are all the Chinese characters of Class A and Class B, over 260 of Class C and Class D characters and 20 not included in the guidelines (such as "翰", "韩" and "酪"). In *Reading and Writing Chinese Characters* 780 Chinese characters are taught, among which about 630 are of Class A characters, over 120 of Class B characters and a few of Class C and Class D characters as radicals.

Reading and Writing Chinese Characters has 25 lessons and *From Characters to Words*, 30. Each of the lessons takes 2 hours to teach.

Reading and Writing Chinese Characters is equipped with a workbook and *From Characters to Words* with CDs.

Zhang Huifen
Beijing Language and Culture University
June 2005

目 录
CONTENTS

C
O
N
T
E
N
T
S

第一课

汉字园地
Corner for Chinese Characters

1. 古	gǔ	ancient
古老	gǔlǎo	ancient
2. 故	gù	incident
故事	gùshi	story
3. 姑	gū	girl; aunt
姑姑	gūgu	father's sister; aunt
4. 估	gū	estimate
估计	gūjì	estimate
5. 苦	kǔ	bitter; suffering
刻苦	kèkǔ	hardworking
痛苦	tòngkǔ	pain
6. 奇	qí	queer
奇怪	qíguài	queer
好奇	hàoqí	curious
7. 寄	jì	post
寄信	jì xìn	post a letter
8. 纪	jì	age
年纪	niánjì	age
9. 主	zhǔ	master
主要	zhǔyào	main

	主意	zhǔyi	idea
	主人	zhǔrén	master
10.	运	yùn	carry;luck;fate
	运动	yùndòng	physical exercise;sport
	运气	yùnqi	luck
11.	讨	tǎo	ask for
	讨论	tǎolùn	discuss
12.	论	lùn	speak/write on
	论文	lùnwén	paper
13.	计	jì	calculate
	计划	jìhuà	plan
	计算	jìsuàn	compute
14.	许	xǔ	allow;promise;perhaps
	许多	xǔduō	many
	也许	yěxǔ	perhaps
	不许	bùxǔ	not allow
15.	宴	yàn	feast
	宴会	yànhuì	banquet
16.	宫	gōng	palace
	故宫	gùgōng	the Palace Museum
17.	客	kè	guest
	客人	kèrén	guest
	客气	kèqi	polite;modest
	客厅	kètīng	sitting room
18.	实	shí	solid;true;fact
	真实	zhēnshí	true
	实现	shíxiàn	come ture
	其实	qíshí	in fact
	事实	shìshí	fact
19.	姨	yí	aunt
	阿姨	āyí	aunt
20.	娘	niáng	mother

姑娘	gūniang	girl
21.底	dǐ	bottom
底下	dǐxia	at the bottom
到底	dàodǐ	finally, after all
22.低	dī	low
低声	dīshēng	in a low voice
23.富	fù	rich
富有	fùyǒu	rich
24.福	fú	good fortune
幸福	xìngfú	happiness
25.辛	xīn	hard
辛苦	xīnkǔ	hard
26.幸	xìng	lucky; fortunate
幸运	xìngyùn	lucky, fortunate
27.提	tí	lift
提高	tígāo	raise
提前	tíqián	in advance
28.静	jìng	tranquility
安静	ānjìng	quiet
29.亿	yì	hundred million
一亿	yí yì	a hundred million
30.艺	yì	art
工艺品	gōngyìpǐn	handicrafts
31.忆	yì	recall
回忆	huíyì	recall
记忆力	jìyìlì	the faculty of memory
32.挺	tǐng	rather
挺好	tǐng hǎo	rather good
33.庭	tíng	hall
家庭	jiātíng	family

34.	怕	pà	fear
	可怕	kěpà	terrible
35.	拍	pāi	pat
	拍照	pāi zhào	take a photo
36.	馒	mán	
	馒头	mántou	steamed bun; steamed bread
37.	术	shù	technique
	艺术	yìshù	art
38.	丰	fēng	abundant
	丰富	fēngfù	rich

记忆窍门

Tips for Memorizing Work

一 形声字声旁记忆

Memorize the following characters with the given phonetic elements.

mother's younger sister- ayi
bomu - father's oldest sister

古 gǔ

(ˇ)	古	ancient	古老	gǔlǎo	ancient
(ˋ)	故	incident	故事	gùshi	story
(ˉ)	姑	aunt	姑姑	gūgu	aunt *father's younger sister*
(ˉ)	估	estimate	估计	gūjì	estimate
(kǔ)	苦	bitter; suffering	刻苦	kèkǔ	hardworking
			痛苦	tòngkǔ	pain

奇 qí

( )	骑	*qí mǎ qí zì xíng chē*				*chē kù garage*
(ˊ)	奇	queer	奇怪	qíguài	queer	*yǒu yòng- helpful*
			好奇	hàoqí	curious	*yóu yǒng- swimming*

jīng qí / jīng yà - surprise

【注】　给"骑"注音、组词，给词组注音。该字已学过，放在此处是为了以旧字带新字，以新字复习旧字。以下画线部分与此相同。

Mark "骑" with phonetic symbols, form phrases with it and mark the phrases with phonetic symbols. Do the same with the following underlined parts.

寄　jì

(`)　寄　post　　　　　　　寄信　jì xìn　　post a letter
(   )　椅　<u>yǐ zi (chair)</u>

己　jǐ

(   )　记　<u>jì de (remember)</u>
(`)　纪　age　　　　　　　年纪　niánjì　　age
(   )　起　<u>qǐ (dui bu qǐ – sorry)</u>

主　zhǔ

(ˇ)　主　master　　　　　主要　zhǔyào　　main
　　　　　　　　　　　　　　主意　zhǔyi　　　idea
　　　　　　　　　　　　　　主人　zhǔrén　　master – host
(   )　住　<u>zhù – to live</u>
(   )　注　<u>zhù yì – pay attention</u>

云　yún

(`)　运　carry; luck; fate　　运动　yùndòng　physical exer-cise, sport
　　　　　　　　　　　　　　运气　yùnqi　　　luck

古	故	姑	估	苦	奇	寄	纪	主	运

二　形声字形旁记忆

Memorize the following characters with the given pictographic elements.

讠—	讨	tǎo	ask for	讨论	tǎolùn	discuss
	论	lùn	speak/write on	论文	lùnwén	paper
	计	jì	calculate	计划	jìhuà	plan
				计算	jìsuàn	compute
	许	xǔ	allow;promise; perhaps	许多	xǔduō	many
				也许	yěxǔ	perhaps
				不许	bùxǔ	not allow
宀—	宴	yàn	feast	宴会	yànhuì	banquet
	宫	gōng	palace	故宫	gùgōng	the Palace Museum
	客	kè	guest	客人	kèrén	guest
				客厅	kètīng	sitting room
				客气	kèqi	polite;modest
	实	shí	solid;true;fact	真实	zhēnshí	true
				实现	shíxiàn	come true
				其实	qíshí	in fact
				事实	shìshí	fact
女—	姨	yí	aunt	阿姨	āyí	aunt
	娘	niáng	mother	姑娘	gūniang	girl

讨	论	计	许	宴	宫	客	实	姨	娘

三　比较下列形近字

Compare the following characters with similar pictographic elements.

底—低

底	dǐ	bottom	底下	dǐxia	at the bottom
			到底	dàodǐ	finally;after all

低	dī	low	低声	dīshēng	in a low voice

富——福

富	fù	rich	富有	fùyǒu	rich
福	fú	good fortune	幸福	xìngfú	happiness

辛——幸

辛	xīn	hardship	辛苦	xīnkǔ	hard
幸	xìng	luck	幸运	xìngyùn	luck, fortunate

提——题

提	tí	raise	提高	tígāo	raise
			提前	tíqián	in advance
题		_____			

净——静

净		_____			
静	jìng	quiet	安静	ānjìng	quiet

亿——艺——忆

亿	yì	hundred million	一亿	yí yì	a hundred million
艺	yì	art	工艺品	gōngyìpǐn	handicrafts
忆	yì	recall	回忆	huíyì	recall
			记忆力	jìyìlì	the faculty of memory

挺——庭

挺	tǐng	rather	挺好	tǐng hǎo	rather good
庭	tíng	hall	家庭	jiātíng	family

怕——拍

怕	pà	fear	可怕	kěpà	terrible
拍	pāi	pat	拍照	pāi zhào	take a photo

慢——馒

慢		_____			

馒　mán　　　　　　馒头　mántou　steamed bun；steamed bread

木——术

　　木　_____

　　术　shù　technique　艺术　yìshù　　　art

王——丰

　　王　_____

　　丰　fēng　abundant　丰富　fēngfù　　　rich

底	低	富	福	辛	幸	提	静	亿	艺	忆	挺	庭	怕
拍	馒	术	丰										

活用园地
Corner for Flexible Usage

一　组词

Form words and phrases.

古　ancient：
　　古人　ancient figures　古怪　odd　古典（diǎn）classical
　　古文　ancient Chinese prose　自古以来　since ancient times

故　incident；on purpose：
　　故意　intentional　事故　accident　故乡　home place
　　故居　former residence

姑　aunt：
　　姑妈　paternal aunt　姑父　uncle

估　estimate：
　　低估　underestimate　估算　estimate

苦　bitter；suffering：
　　苦难（nàn）misery　吃苦　suffer　苦干　work hard

苦笑　forced smile

奇　queer：

好奇心　curiosity　千奇百怪　all kinds of strange things

寄　post：

邮寄　post　寄钱　send money　寄放　leave with

纪　age：

世纪　century　纪念　in commemoration of
纪念日　commemoration day　纪念品　souvenir

主　master；host；God；main：

主动　on one's own initiative　主观　subjective　主张　advocate
主食　staple food　女主人　hostess　主语　subject　民主　democracy
天主教　catholic church

运　carry；luck：

运动会　sports meet　运动员　sportsman of sportswoman
运用　utilize　运行　move　运送　transport

讨　ask for：

商讨　discuss

论　speak on：

不论　no matter what，how，etc.　论点　argument

计　calculate：

计算机　computer　会计　accountant　温度计　thermometre
计较　fuss about

许　allow；promise；perhaps：

不许　no permission　许可　permit　许愿　promise sb. a reward
或许　maybe　准许　allow；permit

宴　feast：

晚宴　dinner party　午宴　luncheon　宴请　entertain(to dinner)

宫　palace：

皇(huáng)宫　imperial palace　少年宫　children's palace
文化宫　caltural palace　白宫　the White House

客　guest：

请客　entertain guests　顾客　customer　旅客　traveller
游客　tourist　客观　objective　房客　boarder
好客　be hospitable　客户　client

实　solid：

说实话　tell the truth　事实　fact　老实　honest
实习　do field work　实用　practical　实力　strength
实行　carry out　实在　indeed　实况　what is actually happening
实事求是　seek truth from facts

娘　mother：

老大娘　old woman；grandma　新娘　bride

底　bottom：

底片　photographic plate；negative　月底　the end of the month
年底　the end of the year

低　low：

低级　vulgar　低头　lower one's head
低下　(of status)low；humble　低温　low temperature

富　rich：

富人　rich people　富足　abundant　富贵　riches and honor

福　happiness：

祝福　wish happiness to　福气　fortune　福建　Fujian
福州　Fuzhou(city)

辛　hard：

千辛万苦　all kinds of hardships　辛酸　miserable；sad

幸　lucky：

不幸　unfortunate　幸好　as luck would have it　幸福　happiness

提　raise；suggest：

提出　put forward；pose　提问　raise a question　提醒　remind
手提包　handbag　提交　refer to；submit　提示　prompt
提议　propose　提早　advance

静　quiet：

冷静　calm　平静　peaceful and quiet　静止　tranquil

亿　hundred million：

亿万　hundreds of millions

艺　art：

文艺　literature and art　手艺　skill　球艺　ball game skills
艺术品　work of art　艺术家　artist

忆　recall：
　　记忆　memorize

挺　erect；endure；rather：
　　挺立　stand upright　挺得住　endure　挺冷　rather cold

庭　front yard；law court：
　　庭院　courtyard　法庭　law court

怕　fear；I suppose：
　　怕死(sǐ)　fear death　恐(kǒng)怕　perhaps

拍　clap；take(a picture)：
　　拍球　bounce a ball　拍电影　make a film　拍卖　auction
　　拍手　clap one's hands；applaud　拍子　racket

术　skill：
　　美术　fine arts　武术　martial art　手术　operation
　　术语　term　艺术品　work of art

丰　abundant
　　丰收　good harvest　丰产　good harvest
　　丰衣足食　have ample food and clothing

二　认读句子

Read and try to understand the following sentences.

1. 中国是一个古老的国家，有 13 亿人口。
   China is a country with a long history, and has a population of 1.3 billion.

2. 这是一个真实的故事。
   This is a true story.

3. 宴会上客人很多，我估计有 100 多人。
   There are many guests at the banquet. I think there may be over a hundred of them.

4. 那位老人年纪很大，记忆力不行了。
   That old man is in his advanced years, and his memory is failing.

5. 常常听录音，可以提高汉语水平。
   It will help to improve your Chinese to listen to the recording very often.

6. 我不太了解他的家庭情况。
   I do not know much about his family.

7. 他很<u>富有</u>,没有姐妹,也没有兄(xiōng)弟。

   He is rich, and he has no brothers or sisters.

8. <u>奇怪</u>,今天这儿怎么这么<u>安静</u>?

   How strange! Why is it so quiet?

9. 请<u>安静</u>,我听不清楚老师的讲话了。

   Please keep quiet. I cannot hear the teacher clearly.

10. 大家一般都来这个商店买东西,<u>主要</u>是因为这儿的商品很<u>丰富</u>,还不太贵。

    People often come to this store for shopping mainly because there are abundant goods here and they are not too expensive.

11. 他去<u>寄信</u>了,马上回来,他让你在这儿等他。

    He has gone to post a letter and will be back in a minute. He asked you to wait for him here.

12. 我有一个旅行<u>计划</u>,我准备夏天的时候去上海和广州。

    I have a travel plan. I am going to Shanghai and Guangzhou this summer.

13. 昨天我去小王家<u>做客</u>,他爸爸、妈妈对我很热情。

    I went to visit Xiao Wang's family yesterday. His parents were very kind to me.

14. 山本在<u>艺术系</u>学习。

    Mayamoto studies in the art department.

15. 祝你<u>幸福</u>快乐。

    Wish you happiness.

16. 这儿很<u>安静</u>,我们就在这儿讨论<u>论文</u>吧。

    It is very quiet here. Let's discuss the paper here.

17. 足球在桌子<u>底下</u>。

    The football is under the table.

18. 老张又住院了,<u>主要</u>是心脏有问题。

    Lao Zhang is hospitalized again. He has trouble with his heart.

19. 万老师很喜欢<u>运动</u>,我常常看见他在操场锻炼身体。

    Professor Wan loves sports. I often see him do physical exercise on the sports ground.

20. 她姐姐是医生,工作挺<u>辛苦</u>的。

    Her elder sister is a doctor and works hard.

21. 昨天我去书店买词典，真幸运，我买到了最后一本。
I went to the bookshop to buy the dictionary. I was lucky enough to get the last copy.

22. 回国的时候，我想带一些中国的工艺品给我的朋友。
I would like to bring back some Chinese handicraft articles to my friends when I go back.

23. 夏子低声问我："这个句子怎么念？"
Xiazi asked me in a low voice, "How should I read this sentence?"

24. "到底什么是幸福？"也许每个人的回答都不一样。
What in the world is happiness? Perhaps different people have different answers.

25. 女主人很客气地把客人迎进了客厅。
The hostess led the guest courteously to the sitting room.

26. 他爸爸月底来北京，想来看看故宫和长城。
His father will come to Beijing at the end of the month to visit the Palace Museum and the Great Wall.

27. 许多年轻姑娘都想让自己看起来瘦一点儿。
Many young girls are eager to look thinner.

28. 这个主意其实不是我想出来的，是那个小姑娘告诉我的，你没想到吧？
In fact, this idea is not mine and I was told by that girl. It's out of your expectation, isn't it?

29. 我原来打算毕业以后先工作一两年再来中国，现在这个愿望提前实现了。
I planned to work for one or two years after my graduation before coming to China. Now the dream has come true ahead of schedule.

30. 他不会游泳，从小就怕水。
He does not swim and he is afraid of water since childhood.

31. 你拍的照片真漂亮。
The photo you took is really beautiful.

32. 她哥哥很会唱歌，大家听了都拍手叫好。
Her elder brother is good at singing. Everybody applauded after they heard him sing.

自学园地
Corner for Self-study

一 给下列词语注音
Mark the following words with phonetic symbols.

故事　　　　痛苦　　　　幸福　　　　计划　　　　年纪
(　　　)　(　　　)　(　　　)　(　　　)－(　　　)

家庭　　　　实现　　　　奇怪　　　　讨论　　　　安静
(　　　)　(　　　)　(　　　)　(　　　)　(　　　)

二 组词
Form words and phrases.

1. 客：＿＿＿　＿＿＿　4. 提：＿＿＿　＿＿＿
2. 许：＿＿＿　＿＿＿　5. 运：＿＿＿　＿＿＿
3. 苦：＿＿＿　＿＿＿　6. 主：＿＿＿　＿＿＿

三 写出本课含有下列偏旁的汉字
Write out the characters with the following elements in this lesson.

宀：(jì)＿＿信　　　　(yàn)＿＿会　　　　故(gōng)＿＿
　　(kè)＿＿人　　　　(shí)＿＿现　　　　(fù)＿＿有
讠：(jì)＿＿算　　　　(xǔ)＿＿多　　　　(tǎo)＿＿论
女：(gū)＿＿娘　　　　阿(yí)＿＿
艹：辛(kǔ)＿＿　　　　(yì)＿＿术
亻：(gū)＿＿计　　　　高(dī)＿＿　　　　(yì)＿＿万
扌：(tǐng)＿＿好　　　　(pāi)＿＿照
忄：回(yì)＿＿　　　　可(pà)＿＿

四　选择填空

Choose the right characters to fill in the blanks.

1. 那位老人不太_____有,可是他觉得很幸_____,因为他的孩子们对他
   很好。　　　　　　　　　　　　　　　　　　　　　　　　　　　　(福、富)

2. 老师,我可以_____一个问_____吗?　　　　　　　　　　　(提、题)

3. 爸爸在儿子头上_____了一下,说:"别_____,再来一次!"　(怕、拍)

4. 这个地方不错,很干_____,也很安_____。　　　　　　　　(静、净)

5. 床_____下很脏。　　　　　　　　　　　　　　　　　　　　(底、低)

6. 年_____大了,_____忆力不行了。　　　　　　　　　　　(纪、记)

7. 我很喜欢这些艺_____品。　　　　　　　　　　　　　　(木、术、禾、米)

8. 我_____在 33 楼 308 号,有时间来我家_____客。

   　　　　　　　　　　　　　　　　　　(注、往、住)(故、做、估)

9. 天_____了。人的心_____也好起来了。　　　　　　　(晴、请、情、清)

10. 你喜欢_____动吗?　　　　　　　　　　　　　　　　(云、会、层、运)

五　选择合适的词填空

Choose the right words to fill in the blanks.

1. 辛苦　　痛苦　　刻苦
   (1)他爸爸开出租车,每天工作都很_____。
   (2)小姑娘经过_____的努力,在学校运动会上取得了冠军。
   (3)这个病给他妈妈带来了很大的_____。

2. 真实　　其实
   (1)你别听他的,他一点儿也不了解_____的情况。
   (2)你别听他的,_____他并不了解这儿的情况。

3. 许多　　很多
   (1)每天来这儿游玩的人_____。
   (2)_____人都会来到这里游玩、拍照。

4. 幸运　　运气
   (1)我真_____,遇上了这么一位好老师。
   (2)你真有_____,遇上了一位好姑娘。

第二课

汉字园地
Corner for Chinese Characters

1.	晴	qíng	sunny
	晴天	qíngtiān	sunny day
2.	飘	piāo	wave
	飘扬	piāoyáng	flutter
3.	永	yǒng	eternal
	永远	yǒngyuǎn	always
4.	梨	lí	pear
	梨树	lí shù	pear tree
5.	证	zhèng	proof; certificate
	证明	zhèngmíng	prove; proof
	身份证	shēnfènzhèng	ID card
	签证	qiānzhèng	visa
6.	政	zhèng	administrative; domestic affairs
	政治	zhèngzhì	politics
7.	整	zhěng	whole; put in order
	整齐	zhěngqí	tidy
8.	裹	guǒ	wrap
	包裹	bāoguǒ	parcel

9.	棵	kē	(a measure word for trees, etc.)
	一棵树	yì kē shù	a tree
10.	颗	kē	(a measure word for anything small and roundish)
	一颗星	yì kē xīng	a star
11.	台	tái	platform; table broadcasting station
	阳台	yángtái	balcony
	电台	diàntái	radio station
	电视台	diànshìtái	television station
12.	抬	tái	raise; lift
	抬头	tái tóu	raise one's head
13.	吉	jí	lucky
	吉利	jílì	lucky
14.	结	jié	settle; finish
	结果	jiéguǒ	result
	结束	jiéshù	come to end
15.	洁	jié	clean
	洁白	jiébái	clean and white
16.	握	wò	hold
	握手	wò shǒu	shake hands
17.	挂	guà	hang
	挂号	guà hào	register
18.	扰	rǎo	disturb
	打扰	dǎrǎo	disturb
19.	拾	shí	pick up
	收拾	shōushi	put in order
20.	技	jì	skill
	技术	jìshù	technique
	杂技	zájì	acrobatics

21. 排	pái	row;form a row
排球	páiqiú	volleyball
安排	ānpái	arrange
22. 亮	liàng	bright
月亮	yuèliang	the moon
23. 夜	yè	night
半夜	bànyè	midnight
24. 产	chǎn	produce
生产	shēngchǎn	produce;production
产生	chǎnshēng	come into being
产品	chǎnpǐn	product
产量	chǎnliàng	output
25. 喂	wèi	(of greeting)hello;feed
26. 咱	zán	(dialect) I or me
咱们	zánmen	(dialect) we or us
27. 恋	liàn	be obsessed with
恋爱	liàn'ài	be in love with
网恋	wǎngliàn	online love affair
28. 恐	kǒng	fear
恐怕	kǒngpà	be afraid
恐怖	kǒngbù	terror
29. 辅	fǔ	assist
辅导	fǔdǎo	coach
30. 傅	fù	teach
师傅	shīfu	master
31. 查	chá	inspect
检查	jiǎnchá	inspect
32. 扬	yáng	raise
表扬	biǎoyáng	commend praise
33. 治	zhì	cure
治病	zhì bìng	cure a disease

34.	活	huó	live; active; work
	生活	shēnghuó	life
	活动	huódòng	exercise; activity
35.	检	jiǎn	inspect
	检讨	jiǎntǎo	self-criticism
36.	叉	chā	fork
	叉子	chāzi	fork
37.	义	yì	meaning
	意义	yìyì	significance
38.	兄	xiōng	elder brother
	兄弟	xiōngdì	brother

记忆窍门

Tips for Memorizing Work

一 形声字声旁记忆

Memorize the following characters with the given phonetic elements.

青　qīng

（　）请　_____

（　）青　_____

（　）情　_____

（ˊ）晴　sunny　　　晴天　qíngtiān　　　sunny day

（　）精　_____

（　）睛　_____

（　）猜　_____

票　piào

（　）漂　_____

		（ˉ） 飘	wave	飘扬	piāoyáng	flutter
永	yǒng					
		（ ） 泳				
		（ˇ） 永	eternal	永远	yǒngyuǎn	always
利	lì					
		（ˊ） 梨	pear	梨树	lí shù	pear tree
正	zhèng					
		（ˋ） 证	proof；certificate			
				证明	zhèngmíng	prove；proof
				身份证	shēnfènzhèng	ID card
				签证	qiānzhèng	visa
		（ˋ） 政	administrative/domestic affairs			
				政治	zhèngzhì	politics
		（ˇ） 整	whole；put in order			
				整齐	zhěngqí	tidy
果	guǒ					
		（ˇ） 裹	wrap	包裹	bāoguǒ	parcel
		（kē） 棵	a measure word for tree，etc.			
				一棵树	yì kē shù	a tree
		（kē） 颗	a measure word for anything small and roundish			
				一颗星	yì kē xīng	a star
台	tái					
		（ˊ） 台	platform；table			
				阳台	yángtái	balcony
				电台	diàntái	radio station
				电视台	diànshìtái	television station
		（ˊ） 抬	raise；lift	抬头	tái tóu	raise one's head
吉	jí					
		（ˊ） 吉	lucky	吉利	jílì	lucky
		（jié） 结	settle；finish			

	结果	jiéguǒ	result
	结束	jiéshù	end；finish
(jié) 洁 clean	洁白	jiébái	clean and white

屋 wū

( ) 屋 _____

| (wò) 握 hold | 握手 | wò shǒu | shake hands |

晴	飘	永	梨	证	政	整	裹	棵	颗	台	抬	吉	结

洁	握

二 形声字形旁记忆

Memorize the following characters with the given pictographic elements.

扌——挂	guà	hang	挂号	guà hào	register
扰	rǎo	disturb	打扰	dǎrǎo	disturb
拾	shí	pick up	收拾	shōushi	put in order
技	jì	skill	技术	jìshù	technique
			杂技	zájì	acrobatics
排	pái	row；form a row	排球	páiqiú	volleyball
			安排	ānpái	arrange
亠——亮	liàng	bright	月亮	yuèliang	the moon
夜	yè	night	半夜	bànyè	midnight
产	chǎn	produce	生产	shēngchǎn	produce
			产生	chǎnshēng	come into being
			产品	chǎnpǐn	product
			产量	chǎnliàng	output
口——喂	wèi	(of greeting)hello；feed			
咱	zán	(dialect) I or me	咱们	zánmen	(dialect) we or us
心——恋	liàn	be obsessed with	恋爱	liàn'ài	be in love with
			网恋	wǎngliàn	online love affair

恐　kǒng　fear　　　　　恐怕　kǒngpà　　be afraid
　　　　　　　　　　　　　恐怖　kǒngbù　　terror

挂　扰　拾　技　排　亮　夜　产　喂　咱　恋　恐

三　比较下列形近字

Compare the following characters with similar pictographic elements.

辅——傅

辅　fǔ　assist　　　　　辅导　fǔdǎo　　coach
傅　fù　teach　　　　　　师傅　shīfu　　master

香——查

香　_____
查　chá　inspect　　　　检查　jiǎnchá　　inspect

场——扬

场　_____
扬　yáng　raise　　　　　表扬　biǎoyáng　　praise

抬——治

抬　_____
治　zhì　cure　　　　　　治病　zhì bìng　　cure a disease

话——活

话　_____
活　huó　live　　　　　　生活　shēnghuó　　life
　　　　　　　　　　　　　活动　huódòng　　exercise; activity

脸——检

脸　_____
检　jiǎn　inspect　　　　检讨　jiǎntǎo　　self-criticism

叉——义

叉　chā　fork　　　　　　叉子　chāzi　　fork
义　yì　meaning　　　　　意义　yìyì　　significance

况——兄

况 _____

兄 xiōng   elder brother   兄弟 xiōngdì   brother

辅 傅 查 扬 治 活 检 叉 义 兄

活用园地

Corner for Flexible Usage

一　组词

Form words and phrases.

飘　　wave：
　　飘动 float（in the air）　飘舞 sway

永　　eternal：
　　永别 farewell　永久 permanent

证　　proof；certificate：
　　学生证 student ID card　工作证 employee ID card
　　证件 document　证书 diploma　出生证 birth certificate
　　许可证 permit　证实 confirm

政　　administrative/domestic affairs：
　　邮政 post　内政 internal affairs　行政 administration
　　政府（fǔ）government　政策（cè）policy　政变 coap d'état

整　　whole；put in order：
　　整个 complete　整整齐齐 tidy　整天 all day long
　　完整 complete　整体 entirety　整数 integer

台　　platform；table：
　　窗台 windowsill　舞台 stage　台风 typhoon
　　上台 go on stage　下台 go off stage　站台 platform
　　写字台 desk　电视台 TV station

吉 lucky：

吉他 guitar 吉日 lucky day

结 settle；finish：

结合 combine 结论 conclusion 结尾 ending

结业 complete a course 结算 settle accounts

洁 clean：

清洁 clean 整洁 clean and tidy

挂 hang：

挂念 miss 挂号室 registration room

扰 disturb：

干扰 interfere

技 skill：

杂技 acrobatics 技能 skills and ability 技巧(qiǎo) skill

科技 science and technology

排 row；form a row：

排队 line up 排练 rehearse 排骨 spareribs 牛排 beefsteak

亮 bright：

明亮 bright 亮光 light

夜 night：

夜晚 night 夜里 at night 夜间 at night 夜班 night shift

夜总会 nightclub 夜市 night market 开夜车 work late into the night

产 produce：

特产 special product 产生 produce 产物 product

产地 place of production 产业 estate 破产 bankruptcy

喂 hello；feed：

喂，你去哪儿了？ Hello，where have you been?

喂奶 feed milk 喂食 feed

恋 be obsessed with：

谈恋爱 be in love 失恋 be disappointed in a love affair

恋人 lover 初恋 first love 热恋 be head over heels in love

留恋 be reluctant to leave

恐 fear：

惊恐 fright 恐吓(hè) frighten 争先恐后 strive to be the first

恐龙 dinosaur 恐怖(bù) terror

反恐　crack down on terrorism

辅　assist：

辅助　assist　辅导员　assistant　辅导老师　tutor

查　inspect：

考查　examine　查阅　look up

扬　raise：

发扬　display

名扬天下　become well-known throughout the country/world

治　cure：

治安　public security　自治区　autonomous region

活　live；active；work：

生活费　living expenses　活泼(pō)　lively　活力　vigour

活该　it serves sb. right　家务活　housework

检　inspect：

体检　physical examination

义　meaning：

名义　name　义务　obligation　多义词　polyseme

同义词　synonym　人道主义　humanism　定义　definition

二　认读句子

Read and try to understand the following sentences.

1. 现在<u>证明</u>是我错了，我应该<u>检讨</u>。
   Now It proved I was wrong，and I should do self-criticism.

2. 红色有时候表示<u>吉利</u>的意思。
   Red is sometimes a symbol of luck.

3. 他站在<u>阳台</u>上<u>抬头</u>看看天上，<u>月亮</u>已经出来了。
   Standing on the balcony and raising his head towards the sky，he saw the moon was up.

4. 山本病了，最近脸色一直不太好，他妈妈要他马上回国<u>治病</u>。
   Mayamoto is ill，and he looks awful these days. His mom wants him to go back to his homeland for treatment.

5. <u>打扰</u>一下，你知道 1225 房间在哪儿吗？

Excuse me，do you happen to know where Room 1225 is?

6. 他是个艺术家，不太关心<u>政治</u>。

He is an artist and is not very interested in politics.

7. 我们的生活习惯跟中国人不太一样，我们吃饭用刀子、<u>叉子</u>，中国人用筷子。

We have a different habit from the Chinese people．We eat with forks and knives，whereas they use chopsticks.

8. 他的房间很<u>整齐</u>。

His room is tidy.

9. 张老师已经在北京<u>生活</u>了 20 年。

Professor Zhang has been living in Beijing for 20 years.

10. 我妈妈正在<u>收拾</u>屋子呢。

My mom is tidying up the room.

11. 请给我<u>挂</u>个号，<u>挂</u>外科。

I would like to register at the surgical department.

12. 在汉语里，有的汉字有几种<u>意义</u>，叫做<u>多义</u>词。

In Chinese，some characters have more than one meaning．These characters are called polysemants.

13. 今天老师<u>表扬</u>了他，说他发音不错。

Today the teacher praised him for his good pronunciation.

14. 很多人都喜欢天鹅，喜欢天鹅<u>洁白</u>的羽毛。

A lot of people love swans for their clean and white feather.

15. 看到自己国家的国旗在运动场上<u>飘扬</u>，运动员心里特别高兴。

Watching their national flag fluttering above the gymnasium，the athletes were very happy.

16. 我要寄一个<u>包裹</u>，寄到美国，大概几天能到？

I would like to send a parcel to the United States．How long will it take to get there?

17. 做饭的时候，妈妈在饭里放了几<u>颗</u>豆，所以很香。

When cooking the rice，Mom put a few beans in it，and the cooked rice is really appetizing.

18. 古汉字"友"，像两只手<u>握</u>在一起，表示友好。

The ancient Chinese character"友"，which looks like two hands shaking together，means "friendship".

19. 他们<u>兄弟</u>俩都很喜欢体育<u>活动</u>,他喜欢打篮球,他弟弟喜欢打<u>排球</u>。

The two brothers both like sports. He likes playing basketball, and his younger brother likes playing volleyball.

20. 我们的作业,老师每天都要<u>检查</u>。

The teacher checks our homework every day.

21. 那个工厂今年计划<u>生产</u>100万台电视机。

The factory plans to manufacture one million TV sets.

22. 她年纪太小,<u>半夜</u>醒了,常常会想家。

She is too young. Waking up at midnight, she often misses her family.

23. 你最喜欢什么水果,橘子、苹果还是<u>梨</u>?

What do you like best, the orange, apple or pear?

24. 他是一个网球运动员,<u>技术</u>很好。

He is a tennis player with very good skill.

25. 桌子上面<u>挂</u>着一张地图。

A map hangs above the table.

26. 他们俩正在谈<u>恋爱</u>。

They are in love with each other.

27. 我非常需要一位<u>辅导</u>老师教我语法。

I need badly a tutor who can teach me grammar.

自学园地

Corner for Self-study

一 给下列词语注音

Mark the following words and phrases with phonetic symbols.

政治	签证	结束	特产	打扰
( )	( )	( )	( )	( )
安排	谈恋爱	检查	生活	技术
( )	( )	( )	( )	( )

二 组词

Form words and phrases.

1. 证：_____ _____ 　2. 结：_____ _____ 　3. 排：_____ _____

4. 活：_____ _____ 　5. 意：_____ _____ 　6. 产：_____ _____

7. 整：_____ _____ 　8. 夜：_____ _____

9. 台：_____ _____ 　10. 恋：_____ _____

三 写出本课含有下列偏旁的汉字

Write out the chinese characters with the following elements in this lesson.

扌：(wò)_____手　　(tái)_____头　　打(rǎo)_____　　杂(jì)_____

安(pái)_____　　表(yáng)_____　　(guà)_____号　　收(shi)_____

宀：月(liang)_____　　(chǎn)_____品　　半(yè)_____

氵：整(jié)_____　　(zhì)_____病　　(huó)_____动

木：(jiǎn)_____查　　(lí)_____树　　一(kē)_____树

心：(liàn)_____爱　　(kǒng)_____怕

四 选择填空

Choose the right characters to fill in the blanks.

1. 窗外_____着大雪，大地一片_____白。　　（票、飘、漂）（结、洁、桔、吉）

2. 他爸爸正在南方_____病。　　　　　　　　　（治、始、抬、台）

3. 每个孩子都喜欢得到老师的表_____。　　　（扬、场）

4. 他的学生_____不见了。　　　　　　　　　（正、整、证、政）

5. 这_____树上有很多苹果。　　　　　　　　（课、棵、颗、果、裹）

6. 他_____我忘了，_____经给我打了两次电话了。（怕、拍）（己、已）

7. 老人说，他要_____到老，学到老。　　　　（活、话、刮、适）

8. 你最近_____色不太好，要不要去医院_____查一下？（脸、检）

9. 学习汉语真是太有意_____了。　　　　　　（叉、文、义、又）

10. 她每天都要去游_____。　　　　　　　　　（永、泳）

五　阅读下列句子并回答问题

Read the following sentences and answer the questions accordingly.

1. 喂，请问你找谁？
　　"你"正在做什么？

2. 你寄的<u>包裹</u>大概一个星期能到，这是<u>包裹单</u>，请在这儿写上你的<u>身份证</u>或护照的号码。
　　"你"现在在哪儿？在做什么？

3. 因为有事，比赛还没<u>结束</u>，我就走了。第二天看了<u>电视台</u>的节目才知道比赛的<u>结果</u>。
　　"我"是怎么知道结果的？

4. 刚才看<u>杂技</u>的时候，坐在右边第一<u>排</u>第一个的就是<u>王师傅</u>。
　　王师傅坐在哪儿？

5. 一些男女网民在网上互相聊天，慢慢地<u>产生</u>了感情，发展成了<u>网恋</u>。
　　什么是网恋？

6. 我们工厂<u>生产</u>的牛奶产品品种很多，牛奶<u>产量</u>排在全国首位。
　　"我们"工厂的产品有什么特点？

7. 小亮，这些小鸡一天最少要<u>喂</u>两次，千万别忘了，这件事就<u>交给</u>你了。
　　他把什么事交给小亮了？

8. 天<u>晴</u>了，把这些没干的衣服<u>挂</u>到阳台上去。
　　为什么把衣服挂到阳台上去？

第三课

汉字园地
Corner for Chinese Characters

1.	简	jiǎn	simple
	简单	jiǎndān	simple
2.	究	jiū	find out
	研究	yánjiū	research
3.	评	píng	comment
	批评	pīpíng	criticize
4.	式	shì	style
	各式各样	gè shì gè yàng	various styles
	方式	fāngshì	manner
	正式	zhèngshì	formal
5.	退	tuì	retreat
	退休	tuì xiū	retire
6.	腿	tuǐ	leg
	大腿	dàtuǐ	thigh
7.	毕	bì	finish
	毕业	bì yè	graduate
8.	批	pī	approve
	批准	pīzhǔn	ratify
	大批	dàpī	large quantities of
9.	迷	mí	lost; be fascinated by; fan

迷路	mí lù	lose one's way
球迷	qiúmí	ball game fan
网迷	wǎngmí	Internet buff
10. 谜	mí	mystery; riddle
谜语	míyǔ	riddle
11. 洋	yáng	ocean
海洋	hǎiyáng	ocean
12. 养	yǎng	provide for
养老	yǎnglǎo	provide for the aged
13. 约	yuē	make an appointment
约会	yuēhuì	date
大约	dàyuē	about
14. 哟	yō	oh, (expressing slight surprise)
15. 药	yào	medicine
开药	kāi yào	prescribe
中药	zhōngyào	Chinese medicine
16. 研	yán	study
研究生	yánjiūshēng	postgraduate
研究所	yánjiūsuǒ	research institute
17. 确	què	true; firm
确实	quèshí	true
正确	zhèngquè	correct
18. 碰	pèng	touch
碰见	pèngjiàn	run into
19. 队	duì	team
队员	duìyuán	team member

	队长	duìzhǎng	team leader
20.	除	chú	exclude
	除了	chúle	except; besides
21.	降	jiàng	lower
	下降	xiàjiàng	go down
	降低	jiàngdī	reduce
22.	陆	lù	land
	大陆	dàlù	continent
	陆地	lùdì	land
23.	派	pài	send
	派出所	pàichūsuǒ	local police station
	派对	pàiduì	party
24.	科	kē	subject
	科学	kēxué	science
	牙科	yá kē	dental department
25.	变	biàn	change
	改变	gǎibiàn	change
	变化	biànhuà	change
	变成	biànchéng	become
26.	够	gòu	enough; rather
	足够	zúgòu	enough
	能够	nénggòu	be able to
27.	根	gēn	root(a measure word) (for long and thin objects)
	根本	gēnběn	foundation
28.	无	wú	nil; not; without
	无论	wúlùn	no matter what, how, etc.
	无数	wúshù	countless
29.	久	jiǔ	for a long time
	好久	hǎojiǔ	a very long time

	不久	bùjiǔ	soon
30.	团	tuán	round；group
	团结	tuánjié	unite
	代表团	dàibiǎotuán	delegation
31.	困	kùn	besiege；sleepy
	困难	kùnnan	difficulty
32.	丢	diū	lose
	丢脸	diū liǎn	lose face
33.	令	lìng	command
	命令	mìnglìng	order；command
34.	司	sī	take charge of
	司机	sījī	driver
	公司	gōngsī	company
35.	失	shī	lose
	丢失	diūshī	lose
	失去	shīqù	lose
	失业	shī yè	be unemployed
36.	尤	yóu	particular
	尤其	yóuqí	particularly
37.	与	yǔ	and；with
	与……无关	yǔ…wúguān	have nothing to do with

记忆窍门

Tips for Memorizing Work

一 形声字声旁记忆

Memorize the following characters with the given phonetic elements.

间　jiān

（丶）简　simple　　简单　jiǎndān　　　　simple

九　jiǔ

（ˉ）究　find out　　　研究　yánjiū　　　research

平　píng

（　）平　_____

（　）苹　_____

（ˊ）评　comment　　批评　pīpíng　　　criticize

式　shì

（　）试　_____

（ˋ）式　type　　　　各式各样　gè shì gè yàng　various types

　　　　　　　　　　方式　fāngshì　　　manner

　　　　　　　　　　正式　zhèngshì　　formal

退　tuì

（ˋ）退　retreat　　　退休　tuì xiū　　　retire

（ˇ）腿　leg　　　　　大腿　dàtuǐ　　　　thigh

比　bǐ

（ˋ）毕　finish　　　　毕业　bìyè　　　　graduate

（pī）批　approve　　批准　pīzhǔn　　　ratify

　　　　　　　　　　大批　dàpī　　　　large quantities of

米　mǐ

（ˊ）迷　lost；be fascinated by；fan

　　　　　　　　　　迷路　mí lù　　　　lose one's way

　　　　　　　　　　球迷　qiúmí　　　　ball game fan

　　　　　　　　　　网迷　wǎngmí　　　Internet buff

（ˊ）谜　mystery；riddle　谜语　míyǔ　　　riddle

羊　yáng

（ˊ）洋　ocean　　　　海洋　hǎiyáng　　　ocean

（　）样　_____

（ˇ）养　provide for　养老　yǎnglǎo　　　provide for the agod

约　　yuē

（一）约　make an appointment

约会　yuēhuì　date
大约　dàyuē　about

（yō）哟　oh　哟，你怎么也来了？
Yō, nǐ zěnme yě lái le?
Well, how come you're here, too?

（yào）药　medicine　开药　kāi yào　prescribe
中药　zhōngyào　Chinese medicine

简 究 评 式 退 腿 毕 批 迷 谜 洋 养 约 哟 药

二　形声字形旁记忆

Memorize the following characters with the given pictographic elements.

石——研　yán　study　研究生　yánjiūshēng　postgraduate
研究所　yánjiūsuǒ　research institute

确　què　true　确实　quèshí　true
正确　zhèngquè　correct

碰　pèng　touch　碰见　pèngjiàn　run into

阝——队　duì　team　队员　duìyuán　team member

除　chú　exclude　除了　chúle　except; besides

降　jiàng　lower　下降　xiàjiàng　go down
降低　jiàngdī　reduce

陆　lù　land　大陆　dàlù　continent
陆地　lùdì　land

研 确 碰 队 除 降 陆

三 比较下列形近字

Compare the following characters with similar pictographic elements.

旅——派

旅					
派	pài	send	派出所	pàichūsuǒ	local police station
			派对	pàiduì	party

料——科

料					
科	kē	subject	科学	kēxué	science
			牙科	yá kē	dental department

弯——变

弯					
变	biàn	change	改变	gǎibiàn	change
			变化	biànhuà	change
			变成	biànchéng	become

狗——够

狗					
够	gòu	enough;rather			
			足够	zúgòu	enough
			能够	nénggòu	be able to

跟——根

跟					
根	gēn	root	根本	gēnběn	foundation

元——无

元					
无	wú	nil;not;without			
			无论	wúlùn	no matter what,how,etc.
			无数	wúshù	countless

欠——久

欠 _____

久 jiǔ for a long time

好久 hǎojiǔ a very long time

不久 bùjiǔ soon

团——困

团 tuán round；group

团结 tuánjié unite

代表团 dàibiǎotuán delegation

困 kùn besiege；sleepy

困难 kùnnan difficulty

去——丢

去 _____

丢 diū lose 丢脸 diū liǎn lose face

今——令

今 _____

令 lìng command 命令 mìnglìng order；command

司——同

司 sī take charge of

司机 sījī driver

公司 gōngsī company

同 _____

夫——失

夫 _____

失 shī lose 丢失 diūshī lose

失去 shīqù lose

失业 shī yè be unemployed

尤——龙

尤 yóu particular 尤其 yóuqí particularly

龙 _____

写——与

写 _____

| 与 | yǔ | and; with | 与……无关 | yǔ…wúguān | have nothing to do with |

| 派 | 科 | 变 | 够 | 根 | 无 | 久 | 团 | 困 | 丢 | 令 | 司 | 失 | 尤 | 与 |

活用园地

Corner for Flexible Usage

一 组词

Form words and phrases.

简	简直	almost	简短	brief	简体字	simplified Chinese character
究	讲究	be particular about	研究员	researcher		
评	评比	compare and assess	评论	comment		
式	式样	style	西式	Western style	中式	Chinese style
	老式	old style	新式	new style	正式	formal; official
退	退出	withdraw	退还	return	退步	retrogress	后退	retreat
腿	小腿	shank	火腿	ham		
毕	完毕	finish	毕生	all one's life	毕业生	graduate
	毕业论文	graduate paper	毕业证书	diploma		
批	批改	correct	批发	wholesale	批准	ratify
	大批	large number of	分批	group by group		
迷	迷信	superstition	迷人	charming	迷失	get lost
	影迷	movie fan	歌迷	singing enthusiast	戏迷	opera fan
	着迷	be charmed	入迷	be fascinated		
谜	字谜	riddle about a character word	谜底	key to the riddle		
	谜面	hint to the key of the riddle	猜谜	guess a riddle		
洋	太平洋	the Pacific Ocean	大西洋	the Atlantic Ocean		

印度洋　the Indian Ocean　北冰洋　the Arctic Ocean

养　养成　form (a habit)　养活　provide for　养老金　pension
养老院　old people's home　休养　recuperate　收养　adopt
养父　foster father　养母　foster mother　养子　adopted son
喂养　feed

约　失约　fail to keep an appointment
预约　make an appointment in advance　约定　agree on; appoint
合约　agreement　条约　treaty

药　吃药　take medicine　药店　chemist's shop　西药　Western medicine
医药　medicine　药品　medicine　药房　pharmacy　药片　tablet
药水　liquid medicine　药方　prescription　药物　medicine

研　研讨　discuss　教研室　teaching and research section

确　的确　indeed　明确　clear　精确　precise　准确　accurate
确切　definite　确信　firmly believe　确定　decide

碰　碰巧　by chance

队　部队　troop　排队　line up　军队　troop
球队　(ball game) team　乐队　band

除　除非　unless　除夕　New Year's Eve　排除　get rid of　开除　expel

降　降级　demote　降温　lower the temperature
降水　precipitation　降雨　rainfall

陆　大陆　continent　陆军　army　陆路　land route

派　学派　school

科　科学院　academy of sciences　科研　scientific research
科技　science and technology　本科　undergraduate
内科　department of internal medicine　外科　surgical department
眼科　optic department　文科　liberal arts
妇科　department of gynaecology　教科书　textbook

变　变成　change into　变换　alternate　政变　coup d'etat

够　不够　insufficient　够吃　enough to eat
够花　enough to spend　够用　enough to use
够累的　tired enough　够大的　big enough　够难的　hard enough
够辛苦的　tired enough

根　一根头发　a hair　两根筷子　a pair of chopsticks　树根　root
词根　root of a word

无	无意 unintentional 无关 have nothing to do with 无礼 impolite
	无情 ruthless 无比 imcomparable 无知 ignorant
	无法 no way 无聊 bored 无话可说 have nothing to say
	无能为力 unable to do anything about it
久	长久 long 永久 eternal
团	旅游团 tourist group 艺术团 art troupe 代表团 delegation
	团体 group 团员 member 乐团 orchestra
丢	丢失 lose 丢人 disgrace
令	下令 issue orders 法令 laws and decrees
司	上司 superior 司令 commander
失	失业 unemployment 失学 be unable to go to school
	失事 have an accident 失恋 be disappointed in a love affair
	失约 fail to keep an appointment
与	and;with 与此同时 at the same time 与其 rather than

二　认读句子

Read and try to understand the following sentences.

1. 那个孩子迷路了,后来是派出所的同志带他回家的。
   That boy lost his way and it was a policeman from the local police station who took him home.

2. 这些科学家是研究海洋动物的。
   These scientists study marine animals.

3. 今天我在商店碰见了我的一位朋友,我们俩好久没见了。
   I ran into a friend of mine in a shop today. We had not seen each other for a long time.

4. 我爷爷退休很多年了,现在在家养老呢。
   My grandpa retired many years ago, and lives at home in retirement.

5. 他家生活比较困难,最近为了给他弟弟治病,又欠了不少钱。
   They are in financial difficaltes. They have recently run into a lot more debt for his brother's medical treatment.

6. 这个鞋店确实不错,里面有各式各样的鞋,样子都很好看。
   This is a very good shoe store with various kinds of shoes in elegant style.

7. 我们班全体同学都很<u>团结</u>,大家有<u>困难</u>互相帮助,像一家人一样。

   The students of our class are united, and help each other to get over difficulty. We are like a family.

8. 那个大学已<u>经批准</u>他入学了。

   That university has decided to admit him.

9. <u>无论</u>你怎么说,我也不会<u>改变</u>我的想法。

   Whatever you say, I won't change my mind.

10. 他妹妹今年就要大学<u>毕业</u>了,毕业以后她也想来中国留学。

    His younger sister is going to graduate this year and she wants to study in China.

11. 这个问题很<u>简单</u>,很容易回答。

    It is very easy to answer this simple question.

12. 昨天买的面包<u>足够</u>我们吃两天了。

    The bread we bought yesterday is enough for us to go round for two days.

13. 这<u>些</u>鱼是<u>养不活</u>的,你别买了。

    Don't buy such fish, because you can't keep it alive.

14. 这两天温度<u>下降</u>了,要多穿点儿衣服。

    You have to put on more clothes, as the temperature has gone down these days.

15. 现在我<u>进退两难</u>,你说我应该怎么办。

    What do you say I should do now that I'm in a dilemma?

16. <u>上课</u>的时候,那个孩子不爱回答问题,他觉得说错了很<u>丢脸</u>。

    The boy is reluctant to answer questions in class for he is afraid he will lose face if he makes a mistake.

17. 妈妈常常<u>批评</u>小龙饭前不洗手。

    Mom often criticizes Xiao Long for forgetting to wash his hands before meals.

18. 昨天足球比赛的时候,那个运动员不小心踢到了他的<u>大腿</u>。

    In the football match yesterday, he was kicked in his thigh by accident.

19. 我跟那个<u>司机约</u>好了,下午 3 点他在楼下等我。

    I've told the driver to pick me up downstairs at 3 pm.

20. 我喜欢打球,尤其是排球,我以前是我们国家<u>排球队</u>的<u>队员</u>。

    I like ball games, especially volleyball. I used to be a member of the national volleyball team.

21. 那个<u>代表团</u><u>不久</u>就要回国了。

    The delegation will return to its country soon.

22. 有的动物只能在<u>陆地</u>上<u>生</u>活。

    Some animals live on land only.

23. 在山区,还有一些孩子因为家庭经济<u>困难</u>,<u>失去</u>了上学的机会。

    There are still a number of children in the mountainous region who lose the opportunity to go to school only because of poverty.

24. 下午五点我跟朋友有个<u>约会</u>,大约晚上十点以后才能回来。

    I have an appointment with my friends at 5 pm. So I won't be back until 10 pm.

25. 他很会猜<u>谜语</u>。

    He is good at guessing riddles.

26. 金天成是北京大学中文系的<u>研究生</u>。

    Jin Tiancheng is a postgraduate from the Department of the Chinese Language and Literature of Beijing University.

27. 他妈妈每天<u>除了</u>上班以外,还要做饭、洗衣服、收拾房间,真<u>够</u>累的。

    His mother has to do the cooking, washing and cleaning after every day's work. What a hard life!

28. <u>好久</u>没见,你的<u>变化</u>真大,我都认不出你了。

    Haven't seen you for ages. You've changed a lot and I can hardly recognize you.

29. 大厅里坐满了人,<u>根本</u>找不到座位了。

    The auditorium is packed with people, and you can't find any seat.

30. 这件事<u>确实</u>与她无关。

    She has nothing to do with the matter.

自学园地

Corner for Self-study

一 给下列词语注音

Mark the following words with phonetic symbols.

科学	困难	改变	约会	批评
( )	( )	( )	( )	( )
简单	根本	退休	正确	无论
( )	( )	( )	( )	( )

二　写出本课含有下列偏旁的汉字

Write out characters with the following elements in this lesson.

氵：海（yáng）＿＿＿＿＿　（pài）＿＿＿＿＿出所

石：（què）＿＿＿＿实　（yán）＿＿＿＿究　（pèng）＿＿＿＿见

阝：（duì）＿＿＿＿员　（jiàng）＿＿＿＿低　大（lù）＿＿＿＿　（chú）＿＿＿＿了

辶：（tuì）＿＿＿＿步　网（mí）＿＿＿＿

讠：批（píng）＿＿＿＿　猜（mí）＿＿＿＿语

三　给下列汉字加一笔，变成另一个汉字

Form a new character by adding one stroke to each of the following characters.

古——（　　）　　休——（　　）　　料——（　　）　　王——（　　）

去——（　　）　　木——（　　）　　夫——（　　）　　团——（　　）

今——（　　）　　晴——（　　）　　司——（　　）　　尤——（　　）

四　写出包含下列汉字的字并注音

Write out new characters with the following ones, and mark the new ones with phonetic symbols.

1. 约　／（　　）＿＿＿＿＿　　＼（　　）＿＿＿＿＿

2. 斗　／（　　）＿＿＿＿＿　　＼（　　）＿＿＿＿＿

3. 羊　／（　　）＿＿＿＿＿　　＼（　　）＿＿＿＿＿

4. 比　／（　　）＿＿＿＿＿　　＼（　　）＿＿＿＿＿

5. 米　／（　　）＿＿＿＿＿　　＼（　　）＿＿＿＿＿

6. 句　／（　　）＿＿＿＿＿　　＼（　　）＿＿＿＿＿

五　选择填空

Choose the right characters to fill in the blanks.

1. 他的手机昨天丢了，现在我＿＿＿＿法跟他联系。　　　　（先、元、无）

2. 不知道为什么，我上星期寄给他的信，今天被_____回来了。 （腿、退）

3. 明年他就要_____业了。 （比、毕、批）

4. 她奶奶喜欢_____鸡，一天给它们喂三次食。 （样、养、氧）

5. 对不起，让你_____等了。 （久、欠、夕）

6. 旅游团昨天那个导游病了，这个是新_____来的。 （派、旅）

7. 这个菜里怎么有一_____头发？ （跟、根、很、银）

8. 我要挂一个眼_____。 （可、科、料）

9. 昨天晚上没睡好觉，今天上课的时候，我_____死了。 （困、因、团）

10. _____，我今天忘了吃_____了。 （约、药、哟）

六　阅读下列句子并回答问题

Read the following sentences and answer the questions accordingly.

1. 他已经从中医药研究所正式退休了，但还是有无数的病人找上门来。
   "他"退休以前做什么工作？

2. 昨天，台湾（wān）的第一批农产品已经运到了福建，出现在福州的各大超市。如果台湾和大陆两地能够直接通航，那么这些农产品的价格（jiàgé, price）还能够降低 30%～40%。
   现在为什么不能降低这些台湾农产品的价格？

3. 体育场内，大批的球迷大声地喊着他的名字，为他加油。
   球迷为什么喊着他的名字？

4. 不久前，她在一个派对上认识了一位牙科大夫，最近正忙着约会呢。
   最近"她"在忙什么？

5. 哟，王先生，在公司你是经理，可是现在是在家里，你能不能不用这种命令的方式跟我讲话。
   王先生和说话人可能是什么关系？

6. 最近几年，城市的失业人口多了，大学生毕业以后找工作也变得不是那么容易了，一些大学生就决定考研究生继续学习，因此报考研究生的人数一年比一年多。
   为什么有那么多的人报考研究生？

第四课

汉字园地
Corner for Chinese Characters

1.	护	hù	guard
	护照	hùzhào	passport
2.	达	dá	reach
	到达	dàodá	reach
	达到	dádào	achieve
3.	尺	chǐ	ruler; (a unit of length) 1/3 of a metre
	尺子	chǐzi	ruler
4.	迟	chí	late
	迟到	chídào	be late for
5.	段	duàn	paragraph
	一段话	yí duàn huà	a passage
6.	寸	cùn	(a unit of length) 1/30 metre; small
	尺寸	chǐcùn	size
7.	村	cūn	village
	农村	nóngcūn	countryside
8.	哈	hā	ha
	哈哈大笑	hāhā dà xiào	burst into laughter
	打哈欠	dǎ hāqian	yawn
9.	受	shòu	receive
	接受	jiēshòu	accept
10.	授	shòu	teach

	教授	jiàoshòu	professor
11.	察	chá	examine
	观察	guānchá	observe
	考察	kǎochá	inspect; examine
12.	擦	cā	wipe
	擦桌子	cā zhuōzi	wipe the table
13.	棋	qí	chess
	下棋	xià qí	play chess
14.	基	jī	basis
	基本	jīběn	fundamental
15.	础	chǔ	stone base of a column
	基础	jīchǔ	foundation
16.	验	yàn	examine
	经验	jīngyàn	experience
	实验	shíyàn	experiment
	试验	shìyàn	test
17.	险	xiǎn	danger
	冒险	mào xiǎn	risk
18.	签	qiān	sign
	签证	qiānzhèng	visa
	签字	qiānzì	sign
19.	违	wéi	go against
	违反	wéifǎn	violate
20.	伟	wěi	great
	伟大	wěidà	great
21.	生	shēng	life; grow; raw
	生命	shēngmìng	life
	生物	shēngwù	organism
	生长	shēngzhǎng	grow
	陌生	mòshēng	strange; unfamiliar
22.	死	sǐ	die
	累死了	lèi sǐ le	be exhausted
	死机	sǐjī	crash; go down
23.	熟	shú	familiar; skilled; cooked

熟悉	shúxī	know sb. or sth. well
熟练	shúliàn	skilled
24. 输	shū	lose; transport
输入	shūrù	import; input
25. 赢	yíng	win; gain
赢得	yíngdé	win; gain
26. 深	shēn	deep
深夜	shēnyè	late at night
深入	shēnrù	penetrate into
27. 浅	qiǎn	shallow
浅色	qiǎnsè	light color
28. 粗	cū	crude
粗心	cūxīn	careless
29. 细	xì	fine
细心	xìxīn	careful
30. 宽	kuān	wide
宽大	kuāndà	wide and big
宽带	kuāndài	broad band
31. 窄	zhǎi	narrow
窄小	zhǎixiǎo	narrow and small
32. 厚	hòu	thick
深厚	shēnhòu	profound
33. 薄	báo	thin
薄被子	báo bèizi	thin quilt
34. 软	ruǎn	soft
软件	ruǎnjiàn	software
35. 硬	yìng	hard
硬盘	yìngpán	hard disk
36. 笑	xiào	laugh; laugh at
开玩笑	kāi wánxiào	make a joke
笑话	xiàohua	joke; laugh at
37. 危	wēi	danger
危险	wēixiǎn	danger
危机	wēijī	crisis

记忆窍门
Tips for Memorizing Work

一 形声字声旁记忆

Memorize the following characters with the given phonetic elements.

户　hù

（`）护　guard　　护照　hùzhào　　　　passport

大　dà

（´）达　reach　　到达　dàodá　　　　reach
　　　　　　　　　达到　dádào　　　　achieve

尺　chǐ

（ˇ）尺　a unit of length
　　　　　　　　　尺子　chǐzi　　　　ruler
（´）迟　late　　迟到　chídào　　　　be late for

段　duàn

（　）锻　_____
（`）段　paragraph　一段话　yí duàn huà　a passage

寸　cùn

（`）寸　1/30 metre，small
　　　　　　　　　尺寸　chǐcùn　　　　size
（-）村　village　农村　nóngcūn　　　　countryside

合　hé

（　）盒　_____
（hā）哈　ha　　哈哈大笑　hāhā dà xiào　burst into laughter
　　　　　　　　　打哈欠　dǎ hāqian　　a yawn

受　shòu

 （丶）受　receive　　接受　jiēshòu　　　accept
 （丶）授　teach　　　教授　jiàoshòu　　　professor

察　chá

 （丿）察　examine　　观察　guānchá　　　observe
 　　　　　　　　　　考察　kǎochá　　　　examine；inspect
 （cā）擦　wipe　　　擦桌子　cā zhuōzi　　wipe the table

其　qí

 （　）期　_____
 （　）旗　_____
 （丿）棋　chess　　　下棋　xià qí　　　play chess
 （jī）基　basis　　　基本　jīběn　　　　fundamental

出　chū

 （ˇ）础　stone base of a column
 　　　　　　　　　　基础　jīchǔ　　　　foundation

护	达	尺	迟	段	寸	村	哈	受	授	察	擦	棋	基	础

二　比较下列形近字

Compare the following characters with similar pictographic elements.

脸——验——险——签

 脸　_____

 验　yàn　　　examine　　　经验　jīngyàn　　　experience
 　　　　　　　　　　　　　实验　shíyàn　　　experiment
 　　　　　　　　　　　　　试验　shìyàn　　　test
 险　xiǎn　　　danger　　　冒险　mào xiǎn　　risk
 签　qiān　　　sign　　　　签证　qiānzhèng　　visa
 　　　　　　　　　　　　　签字　qiān zì　　　sign

围——违——伟

围				
违	wéi	go against	违反 wéifǎn	violate
伟	wěi	great	伟大 wěidà	great

验	险	签	违	伟

三 比较下列反义词

Compare the following antonyms.

生——死

生	shēng	life; live; grow	生命	shēngmìng	life
			生物	shēngwù	organism
			生长	shēngzhǎng	grow
死	sǐ	die; extremely	累死了	lèi sǐ le	be exhausted
			死机	sǐjī	crash; go down

生——熟

生	shēng	unripe; uncooked; raw			
			陌生	mòshēng	strange; unfamiliar
熟	shú	familiar; cooked	熟悉	shúxī	know sb. or sth. well
			熟练	shúliàn	skilled

输——赢

输	shū	lost; transport	输入	shūrù	inport
赢	yíng	win; gain	赢得	yíngdé	win; gain

深——浅

深	shēn	deep	深夜	shēnyè	late at night
			深入	shēnrù	penetrate into
浅	qiǎn	shallow	浅色	qiǎnsè	light color

粗——细

粗	cū	crude	粗心	cūxīn	careless
细	xì	fine	细心	xìxīn	careful

宽——窄

宽	kuān	wide	宽大	kuāndà	wide and big
			宽带	kuāndài	broad band
窄	zhǎi	narrow	窄小	zhǎixiǎo	narrow and small

厚——薄

厚	hòu	thick	深厚	shēnhòu	profound
薄	báo	thin	薄被子	báo bèizi	thin quilt

软——硬

软	ruǎn	soft	软件	ruǎnjiàn	software
硬	yìng	hard	硬盘	yìngpán	hard disk

哭——笑

哭					
笑	xiào	laugh；laugh at	开玩笑	kāi wánxiào	make a joke
			笑话	xiàohuà	joke；laugh at

安——危

安					
危	wēi	danger	危险	wēixiǎn	danger
			危机	wēijī	crisis

生	死	熟	输	赢	深	浅	粗	细	宽	窄	厚	薄	软
硬	笑	危											

活用园地
Corner for Flexible Usage

一 组词

Form words and phrases.

护　护士　nurse　爱护　take good care of

达	达到	reach	达成	achieve	表达	express	发达 developed
迟	迟早	sooner or later					
段	一段时间	a period of time	一段路	part of the road			
	一段课文	a passage from the text	手段	means			
寸	英寸	inch	寸步	a single step			
村	村子	village	山村	mountain village	村民	villager	
哈	笑哈哈	laughing	打哈欠	yawn			
受	受到	receive	受气	be bullied	受凉	catch cold	
	受批评	criticized	难受	feel bad	感受	feel	
授	讲授	teach	教授	professor	授课	give lessons	
察	视察	inspect	察看	look into			
擦	擦黑板	clean the blackboard	擦地板	clean the floor			
	擦皮鞋	shine shoes	擦药	apply medicine to			
棋	围棋	*weiqi*	象棋	chess			
基	基地	base	基因	gene	基金	fund	基层 grass-roots
础	经济基础	economic foundation	基础好	good foundation			
	基础差	poor foundation					
验	化验	chemical examination	检验	examine	实验	experiment	
	考验	trial	试验	test			
险	风险	risk	脱险	escape danger			
签	签字	signature	书签	bookmark	牙签	toothpick	
	签名	sign one's name	签到处	sign-in desk			
违	违法	violate the law	违约	violate the agreement			
伟	伟人	great person	伟业	great cause			
生	生动	vivid	生意	business			
死	死心	give up the idea	死活	anyway	该死	damn	
熟	熟人	acqunintance	熟知	know very well			
	熟能生巧	practice makes perfect					
输	输出	export;output	输送	carry;transport			
	输血	blood transfusion					
赢	赢利	profit					
深	深浅	depth	深远	profound and lasting	深色	dark color	
	深刻	deepgoing	加深	strengthen			

深度　depth　深信　firmly believe

粗　粗声粗气　in a deep and gruff voice　粗心大意　careless

粗活　heavy manual labour

细　细小　fine　粗细　thickness　精打细算　careful calculation

宽　宽度　width　宽广　broad　宽容　tolerant

窄　宽窄　width　心眼儿窄　intolerant

厚　厚度　thickness　厚礼　generous gift

深情厚意　profound sentiments of friendship

软　软座　soft seat　心软　be softhearted　手软　be irresolute

软卧(wò)　soft sleeper (on a train)

硬　硬座　hard seat　硬币　coin　硬件　hardware　硬卧　hard sleeper

笑　可笑　ridiculous　好笑　funny　见笑　laugh at　笑容　smile

笑面虎　smiling villain

危　危险品　dangerous article　危机　crisis　危急　critical

病危　be terminally ill

二　认读句子

Read and try to understand the following sentences.

1. 我朋友下午3点到达北京，我要去机场接他。

My friend will arrive in Beijing at 3 p.m., and I'll meet him at the airport.

2. 这一套软件一共多少钱？

How much does this set of software cost?

3. 他这个人喜欢冒险。

He loves adventures.

4. 天气热了，这条被子太厚，我要去买一条薄被子。

It's getting hot. The quilt is too thick and I'll get a thin one.

5. 她习惯穿宽大一点儿的衣服。

She's used to wearing loose clothes.

6. 你学了好几年汉语了，一定有许多好的学习经验。

You've been learning Chinese for years and must have a lot of experience.

7. 他去那个软件公司考察了三次，昨天才决定在合同上正式签字。

He went to the software company to investigate three times. And he didn't decide to formally sign the contract until yesterday.

8. 这条裙子颜色太浅了，请给我换一条深一点儿的。

The color of the skirt is too light. Please give me one in a darker color.

9. 我的书包丢了，护照、签证都在里边。

I've lost my bag, and my passport with visa is in it.

10. 老师说了一段笑话，同学们听了都哈哈大笑。

The teacher told a joke, and the students burst into laughter on hearing it.

11. 他是一个伟大的科学家。

He is a great scientist.

12. 你违反了我们的约定。

You've violated our agreement.

13. 你别听他吹牛，他说的基本上都是假的。

Don't listen to him. What he said are basically lies.

14. 对不起，我迟到了。

I'm sorry that I'm late.

15. 如果你细心观察，就会看出哪个是真的，哪个是假的。

If you observe carefully you will be able to tell the fake from the genuine.

16. 他家在农村，这几年农村的生活也有了很大的改变。

He lives in the countryside. Life in the country has recently changed a lot.

17. 他昨天晚上一直工作到深夜。

He worked late into the night yesterday.

18. 这些都是基础知识，比较容易学。

This is basic knowledge and easy to learn.

19. "熟能生巧"的意思是：只有熟练了才能产生巧办法。

"熟能生巧"means skill comes from practice.

20. 你打电话的时候，她正在擦桌子。

She was cleaning the table when you called.

21. 王教授很喜欢下棋。

Professor Wang loves playing chess.

22. 这个地方又窄又小，我们换一个地方吧。

The place is narrow and small. Let's move to another place.

23. 确实是他错了，所以他接受了大家的批评。

No doubt he was wrong, and he accepted criticism from others.

24. 那棵树很**粗**，这几棵**细**一点儿。
    That is a thick tree, and these ones are not as thick as that one.

25. 我**累**死了，我们休息一会儿再接着爬山吧。
    I'm exhausted. Let's have a rest before we go on.

26. 他是来跟我们**告别**的，他明天回国。
    He's here to say goodbye to us. He's going back to his country tomorrow.

27. 那儿太**危险**了，你别去。
    That's too dangerous. Don't go.

28. 他们兄弟俩感情很**深**。
    The two brothers are closely attached to each other.

29. 我太**粗心**了，我忘了一件很重要的事。
    How careless of me! I forgot one important thing.

自学园地

Corner for Self-study

一 给下列词语注音

Mark the following words with phonetic symbols.

基础	熟悉	危险	观察	护照
（ ）	（ ）	（ ）	（ ）	（ ）

签证	迟到	深浅	硬盘	接受
（ ）	（ ）	（ ）	（ ）	（ ）

二 写出本课含有下列偏旁的汉字并注音

Write out the characters with the following elements in this lesson, and mark them with phonetic symbols.

石：_____（   ）   _____（   ）

犭：_____（   ）   _____（   ）

扌：_____（   ）   _____（   ）   _____（   ）

辶：_____（   ）   _____（   ）   _____（   ）

三　在括号中加上合适的词语

Fill in the blanks with right words and phrases.

接受（　　　　）　　　到达（　　　　　）　　　违反（　　　　　）
输入（　　　　）　　　签订（　　　　　）　　　观察（　　　　　）
深入（　　　　）　　　赢得（　　　　　）

四　写出反义词

Write out the antonyms of the following words and phrases.

近＿＿＿＿＿　　　　　　　　说实话＿＿＿＿＿
哭＿＿＿＿＿　　　　　　　　安全＿＿＿＿＿
深＿＿＿＿＿　　　　　　　　得到＿＿＿＿＿
粗＿＿＿＿＿　　　　　　　　批评＿＿＿＿＿
送＿＿＿＿＿　　　　　　　　进步＿＿＿＿＿
厚＿＿＿＿＿　　　　　　　　上升＿＿＿＿＿
有＿＿＿＿＿　　　　　　　　复杂＿＿＿＿＿
阴＿＿＿＿＿　　　　　　　　直＿＿＿＿＿
宽＿＿＿＿＿　　　　　　　　硬＿＿＿＿＿
生＿＿＿＿＿　　　　　　　　高＿＿＿＿＿

五　选择填空

Choose the right characters to fill in the blanks.

1. 皮鞋脏了,应该＿＿＿＿一下了。　　　　　　　　　　（察、擦）
2. 对不起,今天我有点儿事,所以＿＿＿＿到了。　　　　　（尺、迟）
3. 我喜欢下围＿＿＿＿。　　　　　　　　　　　　　（其、期、棋、旗）
4. 他是在这个＿＿＿＿子里长大的。　　　　　　　　（村、寸、树）
5. 要想学习专业,就要先打好汉语＿＿＿＿础。　　　　（棋、基、期）
6. 昨天晚上他＿＿＿＿了凉,所以今天感冒了。　　　　　（受、授）
7. 他是一个很有名的演员,常常有人请他＿＿＿＿名。　（签、检、验、险）
8. 这一＿＿＿＿课文比较难,请老师讲慢一点儿。　　　　（段、锻）

9. 你也太_____心了，怎么会把护照丢了呢？ （租、粗）
10. 天气冷了，我想去买一条_____巾。 （围、伟、违）

六 **阅读下列句子并回答问题**

Read the following sentences and answer the questions accordingly.

1. 月球上没有<u>生命</u>，那儿既没有空气，也没有水，<u>生物</u>是不可能在那儿<u>生长</u>的。
   月球上有没有生命？为什么？

2. 这个人我对他不太<u>熟悉</u>，虽然以前见过几次面，但对他没有<u>深入</u>的了解。
   "我"为什么对"他"不太熟悉？

3. 在无数次<u>实验</u>的<u>基础</u>上，专家们研究出了一种新的药品，现在正在试用<u>阶段</u>。
   新药品是怎么研究出来的？

4. 最近我家安装(ānzhuāng, install)了<u>宽带</u>，上网快多了，不过，我觉得我现在用的汉字<u>输入</u>方法太慢了，有没有更好更快的汉字<u>输入</u>法，另外，我的电脑老死机是为什么？
   "我"在用电脑方面有什么问题？

5. 你别<u>笑话</u>我了，我哪翻译得了中文小说？我的汉语根本还没<u>达到</u>那么高的水平。
   "我"能不能翻译中文小说？

6. 我刚才困得<u>受不了</u>了，打了好几个哈欠，现在好多了。
   刚才"我"怎么了？

7. 经济<u>危机</u>带来了很多问题，失业人口数量也大大上升。
   为什么失业人口数量上升？

8. 那块牌子上写着，这儿不能游泳，河水深达四五米，在这儿游泳太<u>危险</u>了。
   为什么这儿不能游泳？

9. 昨天的比赛，上海队打得不错，主要是运气不好，最后还是<u>输</u>了，北京队最后<u>赢</u>得了<u>冠军</u>。
   上海队打得怎么样？比赛结果怎么样？为什么？

10. 我对他感到既熟悉又陌生。我们小时候在<u>农村</u>一块儿长大。但是这是他出国八年以后我们第一次见面。
    我对他为什么感到既熟悉又陌生？

第五课

汉字园地
Corner for Chinese Characters

1.	希	xī	hope
	希望	xīwàng	hope
2.	稀	xī	rare
	稀少	xīshǎo	rare
3.	亡	wáng	death
	死亡	sǐwáng	death
4.	望	wàng	gaze into the distance; hope
	失望	shīwàng	be disappointed
5.	且	qiě	even
	而且	érqiě	what is more
6.	组	zǔ	group
	小组	xiǎozǔ	group
	组成	zǔchéng	form
7.	祖	zǔ	originator; ancestor
	祖国	zǔguó	motherland
	祖父	zǔfù	grandfather
	祖母	zǔmǔ	grandmother
	祖先	zǔxiān	ancestor
8.	阻	zǔ	stop
	阻止	zǔzhǐ	stop someone from doing something

9.	织	zhī	weave
	组织	zǔzhī	organization
10.	箱	xiāng	box；case；trunk
	冰箱	bīngxiāng	refrigerator
	邮箱	yóuxiāng	mailbox；postbox
11.	厢	xiāng	box
	车厢	chēxiāng	carriage
12.	乎	hū	
	几乎	jīhū	almost
13.	呼	hū	call
	呼吸	hūxī	breathe
14.	粒	lì	grain
	一粒米	yí lì mǐ	a grain of rice
15.	拉	lā	pull；play
	拉开	lākāi	pull open
	拉拉队	lālāduì	cheering squad
16.	垃	lā	rubbish
	垃圾	lājī	garbage
17.	啦	lā	a verb suffix；suggesting completion of an action
18.	及	jí	and；be in time for
	及时	jíshí	in time
	以及	yǐjí	as well as
	来得及	láidejí	there's still time
	来不及	láibují	there's not enough time
19.	圾	jī	rubbish
	垃圾箱	lājīxiāng	garbage can
20.	总	zǒng	put together；general
	总是	zǒngshì	always
	总结	zǒngjié	summarize；summary

21.	聪	cōng	faculty of hearing
	聪明	cōngmíng	clever
22.	昏	hūn	faint
	头昏	tóu hūn	dizzy
	昏迷	hūnmí	stupor
23.	婚	hūn	marriage
	结婚	jié hūn	wed
	离婚	lí hūn	divorce
24.	任	rèn	official post
	任务	rènwù	task
	任何	rènhé	any
	主任	zhǔrèn	director
25.	偷	tōu	steal
	小偷	xiǎotōu	pilferer
26.	吸	xī	breathe in
	吸烟	xī yān	smoke
	吸取	xīqǔ	absorb
	吸收	xīshōu	assimilate
27.	咬	yǎo	bite
	咬牙	yǎo yá	clench one's teeth(in hatred or pain)
28.	继	jì	succeed to
	继续	jìxù	continue
29.	断	duàn	break
	不断	búduàn	continuous
30.	设	shè	establish
	建设	jiànshè	construct
	设计	shèjì	design
31.	野	yě	wild
	野餐	yěcān	picnic
32.	惜	xī	pity
	可惜	kěxī	what a pity

33. 续	xù	continue
手续	shǒuxù	formality
34. 而	ér	and
因而	yīn'ér	therefore
然而	rán'ér	however
反而	fǎn'ér	on the contrary
35. 器	qì	appliance
机器	jīqì	machine
电器	diànqì	electric appliance
显示器	xiǎnshìqì	display
36. 积	jī	accumulate
面积	miànjī	(land)area
积极	jījí	active

记忆窍门

Tips for Memorizing Work

一 形声字声旁记忆

Memorize the following characters with the given phonetic elements.

希　xī

（一）希　hope　　希望　xīwàng　　hope
（一）稀　rare　　稀少　xīshǎo　　rare

亡　wáng

（　）忘　_____
（ˊ）亡　death　　死亡　sǐwáng　　death
（ˋ）望　gaze into the distance
　　　　　　　失望　shīwàng　　be disappointed

且　qiě

(ˇ)	且	even	而且	érqiě	what is more
( )	姐	_____			
( )	租	_____			
(zǔ)	组	group	小组	xiǎozǔ	group
			组成	zǔchéng	form
(zǔ)	祖	ancestor	祖国	zǔguó	motherland
			祖父	zǔfù	grandfather
			祖母	zǔmǔ	grandmother
			祖先	zǔxiān	ancestor
(zǔ)	阻	stop	阻止	zǔzhǐ	stop

只　zhǐ

( )	职	_____			
(ˉ)	织	weave	组织	zǔzhī	organization

相　xiāng

( )	想	_____			
(ˉ)	箱	box	冰箱	bīngxiāng	refrigerator
			邮箱	yóuxiāng	mailbox；postbox
(ˉ)	厢	box	车厢	chēxiāng	carriage

乎　hū

(ˉ)	乎		几乎	jīhū	almost
(ˉ)	呼	call	呼吸	hūxī	breathe

立　lì

(ˋ)	粒	grain	一粒米	yí lì mǐ	a grain of rice
(lā)	拉	pull	拉开	lākāi	pull open
			拉拉队	lālāduì	cheering squad
(lā)	垃	rubbish	垃圾	lājī	garbage
(lā)	啦	a verb suffix，suggesting completion of an action			
			来啦	lái la	(I'm) coming!

及　　jí

　　(　)　级　_____

　　(　)　极　_____

　　(ˊ)　及　　and；be in time for

及时	jíshí	in time
以及	yǐjí	as well as
来得及	láidejí	there's still time
来不及	láibují	there's not enough time

　　(ˉ)　圾　　垃圾箱　lājīxiāng　garbage can

总　　zǒng

　　(ˇ)　总　put together

总是	zǒngshì	always
总结	zǒngjié	summarize；summary

　　(cōng)　聪　faculty of hearing

　　　　　　聪明　cōngmíng　clever

昏　　hūn

　　(ˉ)　昏　faint

头昏	tóu hūn	dizzy
昏迷	hūnmí	stupor

　　(ˉ)　婚　marriage

结婚	jié hūn	wed
离婚	lí hūn	divorce

希	稀	亡	望	且	组	祖	阻	织	箱	厢	乎	呼	粒
拉	垃	啦	及	圾	总	聪	昏	婚					

二　形声字形旁记忆

Memorize the following characters with the given pictographic elements.

亻——任　rèn　official

任务	rènwù	task
主任	zhǔrèn	director
任何	rènhé	any

　　　　偷　tōu　steal　　小偷　xiǎotōu　pilferer

口——吸　xī　breathe in　吸烟　xī yān　smoke

吸取	xīqǔ	absorb
吸收	xīshōu	assimilate

咬　yǎo　bite　　咬牙　yǎo yá　gnash one's teeth (in hatred or pain)

任	偷	吸	咬

三　比较下列形近字

Compare the following characters with similar pictographic elements.

继——断

继	jì	succeed to		继续	jìxù	continue
断	duàn	break		不断	búduàn	continuous

没——设

没						
设	shè	establish		建设	jiànshè	construct
				设计	shèjì	design

舒——野

舒						
野	yě	wild		野餐	yěcān	picnic

借——惜

借						
惜	xī	pity		可惜	kěxī	what a pity

继	断	设	野	惜

四　基本字带字

Memorize the following characters with basic elements.

卖——续

卖					
续	xù	continue	手续	shǒuxù	formality

而——需

而	ér	and	因而	yīn'ér	therefore
			然而	rán'ér	however
			反而	fǎn'ér	on the contrary

需 _____

哭——器

哭 _____

器	qì	appliance	机器	jīqì	machine
			电器	diànqì	electric appliance
			显示器	xiǎnshìqì	display

只——积

只 _____

| 积 | jī | accumulate | 面积 | miànjī | land area |
| | | | 积极 | jījí | active |

续　而　器　积

活用园地

Corner for Flexible Usage

组词

Form words and phrases.

希　希求 hope for　希望 hope
稀　稀饭 gruel　稀少 rare　稀客 rarely seen visitor
　　稀有 rare　稀薄 thin　古稀 advanced age
亡　灭亡 die　家破人亡 a broken family, with members missing or dead
望　失望 be disappointed　看望 visit　渴望 long for
　　声望 reputation　望远镜 telescope

且	况且 let alone
组	组合 combination 组织 organize
	组长 group leader 词组 phrase
祖	祖先 ancestor 祖父 grandfather 祖母 grandmother
	外祖父 grandpa on the maternal side
	外祖母 grandma on the maternal side
阻	阻力 obstruction 风雨无阻 rain or shine
箱	箱子 box 信箱 letter box 纸箱 paper box
	皮箱 leather suitcase
厢	包厢 special carriage 车厢 carriage
乎	在乎 mind 满不在乎 not worry at all 臭乎乎 a bit off
	胖乎乎 fattish 软乎乎 soft
呼	呼机 caller 欢呼 exclaim 呼救 call for help
	呼叫 call out 呼声 voice
粒	米粒 rice grain 豆粒 bean 一粒药 a pill
拉	拉小提琴（qín）play the violin 拉后腿 hold someone back
	拉关系 cotton up to 拉面 hand-pulled noodle
	拉稀 have loose bowels
垃	垃圾箱 garbage can 垃圾邮件 junk E-mail
啦	来啦 coming 好啦 it's done 行啦 that'll do
及	及早 as soon as possible 及其 and his；hers；its；theirs
	及格（gé）pass an exam
极	好极了 wonderful 高兴极了 extremely happy
	极力 try one's best 北极 the Arctic Pole
	南极 the Antarctic Pole 太极（tàijí）拳 boxing
总	总共 altogether 总和 total 总计 add up to
	总数 sum total 总算 after all 总公司 head office
	总书记 secretary general 总司令 commander in chief
	总得 have to 总的来说 generally speaking
聪	小聪明 clever trick 聪明能干 clever and able
	自作聪明 try to be smart
昏	昏倒 fall down in a faint 昏天黑地 pitch-dark
婚	婚礼 wedding 求婚 suit 金婚 50 years of marriage

	银婚	25 years of marriage	婚外恋	extramarital love		
任	信任	trust	任意	at will	任性	wilful
	上任	take office	任命	appoint		
偷	偷听	eavesdropping	偷看	steal a glance	偷偷	stealthily
吸	呼吸	breathe	吸取	assimilate	吸尘器	vacuum cleaner
咬	咬牙	clench one's teeth				
继	继父	stepfather	继母	stepmother	继子	stepson
	继任	succeed sb. in a post	夜以继日	day and night		
断	打断	interrupt	果断	resolute	断定 decide 片段 excerpt	
	一刀两断	make a clean break				
设	假设	hypothesis	设立	establish	设想	supposition
	设备	equipment	想方设法	try every way		
野	野花	wild flower	野草	weed	野果	wild fruit
	田野	field	野心	wild ambition	野生 wild 野外 field	
惜	爱惜	take good care	不惜	at all cost		
续	陆续	successively	续集	sequel		
而	从而	so	一而再，再而三	again and again	而后	then
	而已	nothing more; only				
器	乐器	music instrument	玉器	jadeware	助听器	hearing aid
	灭火器	fire extinguisher	吸尘器	vacuum cleaner		
积	体积	volume	积累(lěi)	gather		

二　认读句子

Read and try to understand the following sentences.

1. 那个地方人口<u>稀少</u>，有时候<u>几乎</u>看不到人。

   The place is sparsely populated and sometimes you cannot see a soul.

2. <u>忽然</u>，一条狗跑出来<u>咬</u>了我一口。

   All of a sudden，a dog rushed out and gave me a bite.

3. 老师对孩子们说："<u>希望</u>你们好好学习，长大了努力<u>建设</u>伟大的祖国。"

   The teacher said to the children，"I hope you'll work hard and build our country when you grow up."

4. 每次学校<u>组织</u>去旅游，他都很<u>积极</u>。

He is very enthusiastic to participate whenever the school organizes a trip.

5. 她的<u>冰箱</u>总是满满的，你<u>需要</u>什么自己拿吧。

Her refrigerator is always full. Take whatever you need.

6. 爬这么高的山，我的<u>呼吸</u>越来越困难了。

Having climbed so high on the mountain，I found more and more difficult to breathe.

7. 我想借书，<u>需要</u>办什么<u>手续</u>？

I would like to borrow some books. What formalities do I have to go through?

8. 他正在谈恋爱，马上要<u>结婚</u>了。

They are in love with each other，and will get married soon.

9. 要注意不断地<u>吸收</u>国外新的知识，才能做好工作。

We must follow closely and assimilate new knowledge from abroad so that we can do our work better.

10. 你别<u>阻止</u>他，就让他去吧。

Don't try to stop him. Let him go.

11. 他会说英语，<u>而且</u>还会说法语。

He speaks French as well as English.

12. 那个孩子<u>聪明</u>极了。

The boy is very clever indeed.

13. 窗户<u>拉开</u>一点吧，<u>车厢</u>里太热，我有点儿<u>头昏</u>。

Please open the window a bit. It's too hot inside the carriage and I feel a bit dizzy.

14. 做错了，就要<u>及时</u>改正。

One should correct a mistake immediately when having made it.

15. 我们昨天去<u>野餐</u>了，大家玩得很高兴，<u>可惜</u>你没去。

We went for a picnic and enjoyed ourselves. It's a pity that you did not go.

16. 记者说，在那次火灾中，有很多人<u>死亡</u>。

According to the reporter，many people were killed in the fire.

17. 他父母对他很<u>失望</u>。

His parents were disappointed with him.

18. 家里一粒米也没有，让我怎么做饭？你快买米去吧。

There is not a grain of rice left. How can I do the cooking? Go and buy some rice immediately.

19. 这个小组很快就完成了他们的任务。

The group finished their job very soon.

20. 他一直希望到中国来学习，现在真的来啦。

He's been longing to come to study in China. Now he's here at last.

21. 垃圾箱在那边。

The garbage can is over there.

22. 我想继续在这个学校学习，这儿条件不错。

I hope to continue my studies in this school, because conditions here are good.

23. 这个房间面积太小了，能不能换一个大一点儿的。

The room is too small. Can I have a bigger one?

24. 昨天一个小偷偷了他的钱包。

Yesterday a pilferer stole his wallet.

25. 不知道为什么，他的学习没有进步，反而退步了。

He failed to make any progress in his studies, and actually he had lagged behind. I don't know why.

26. 我给你留一个呼机号码，有事你可以呼我。

I'll give you a pager number. Call me when you need my help.

27. 这个孩子胖乎乎的，真可爱。

That plump child is really lovely.

28. 你比赛的时候，我们做你的拉拉队。

When you are in the match, we will be cheering you up.

29. 他每天都锻炼，风雨无阻。

Rain or shine, he does physical exercise every day.

30. 这个工作太困难，而他又是个新手，我们应该帮帮他。

The job is too difficult; what's more, he's a new hand. We should give him a hand.

自学园地

Corner for Self-study

一　给下列词语注音

Mark the following words with phonetic symbols.

祖国　　　　冰箱　　　　机器　　　　可惜　　　　继续
（　　　　）（　　　　）（　　　　）（　　　　）（　　　　）

总结　　　　结婚　　　　希望　　　　积极　　　　聪明
（　　　　）（　　　　）（　　　　）（　　　　）（　　　　）

二　组词

Form words and phrases.

1. 望：＿＿＿　＿＿＿　　2. 祖：＿＿＿　＿＿＿　　3. 而：＿＿＿　＿＿＿
4. 箱：＿＿＿　＿＿＿　　5. 器：＿＿＿　＿＿＿　　6. 吸：＿＿＿　＿＿＿
7. 任：＿＿＿　＿＿＿　　8. 总：＿＿＿　＿＿＿

三　写出本课含有下列偏旁的汉字并注音

Write out the characters with the following elements in this lesson, and mark them with phonetic symbols.

纟：＿＿＿（　　）　　＿＿＿（　　）　　＿＿＿（　　）　　＿＿＿（　　）

口：＿＿＿（　　）　　＿＿＿（　　）　　＿＿＿（　　）　　＿＿＿（　　）

亻：＿＿＿（　　）　　＿＿＿（　　）

禾：＿＿＿（　　）　　＿＿＿（　　）

四 选择填空

Choose the right characters to fill in the blanks.

1. 我希_____你能来参加我们的_____礼。　　　　（望、忘、亡、罔）（昏、婚）
2. 我今天累_____了,想早点儿睡觉。　　　　　　（及、级、极、圾）
3. 他早上习惯吃_____饭,不习惯吃牛奶、面包。　　（稀、希）
4. 那个路口有一个信_____。　　　　　　　　　（想、相、箱、厢）
5. 你_____书还是还书?　　　　　　　　　　　（借、惜、错）
6. 这个地方真脏,垃圾都_____成山了。　　　　　（积、织、职、识）

五 阅读下列句子并回答问题

Read the following sentences and answer the questions accordingly.

1. 我的邮箱里总是会不断地收到一些垃圾邮件,几乎每天都有,真是烦死了。
   什么使"我"很烦?
2. 这个研究小组是由(yóu)各个学校的教授以及研究院的专家组成的。
   研究小组里都有什么人?
3. 这些都是以前的研究者总结出来的成功经验,我们应该及时地吸取这些经验,继续不断地努力。
   这些成功经验是从哪里来的?
4. 房间的面积不大,而家具很漂亮,这些家具都是主人自己设计的。
   这些家具有什么特点?
5. 离婚手续办完后,她不愿意见任何人,因而把自己关在家里,一个星期没出门。
   "她"为什么把自己关在家里不出门。
6. 祖父已经昏迷三天了,祖母每天都要来到床前,拉着祖父的手,静静地看着昏迷不醒的祖父。他们结婚已经六十多年,感情深得让我们这些孙子孙女十分地感动。
   他们为什么感动?
7. 那些东西都是我们祖先留下来的,然而现在都被偷走了。这些小偷让人恨(hèn,hate)得直咬牙。
   "我们"家发生了什么事?
8. "垃圾"这个词现在很常用,什么"垃圾食品"啦、"垃圾邮件"啦、"垃圾时间"啦,用得可多了。
   你知道"垃圾食品""垃圾邮件""垃圾时间"都是什么意思吗?

第六课

汉字园地
Corner for Chinese Characters

1.	倒	①dǎo	fall
	倒下	dǎoxià	fall down
		②dào	pour; move backward
	倒茶	dào chá	pour tea
2.	背	①bēi	carry on one's back
	背包	bēibāo	backpack
		②bèi	back
	背后	bèihòu	behind one's back
3.	烤	kǎo	roast
	烤鸭	kǎoyā	roast duck
4.	拷	kǎo	copy
	拷贝	kǎobèi	copy
5.	董	dǒng	director
	董事长	dǒngshìzhǎng	chairman of the board of directors
6.	态	tài	status
	态度	tàidu	attitude
7.	肤	fū	skin
	皮肤	pífū	skin
8.	扶	fú	support with a hand
	扶手	fúshǒu	handrail

9. 键	jiàn	key
关键	guānjiàn	key
键盘	jiànpán	key board
关键词	guānjiàn cí	keyword
10. 玛	mǎ	
玛丽	Mǎlì	Mary
11. 骂	mà	curse
骂人	mà rén	swear at somebody
12. 议	yì	discuss
会议	huìyì	meeting
建议	jiànyì	suggest
议论	yìlùn	discussion
13. 仪	yí	instrument;ceremony
仪器	yíqì	instrument
14. 阶	jiē	stair
阶段	jiēduàn	stage
15. 价	jià	cost
价钱	jiàqián	price
讨价还价	tǎo jià huán jià	bargain
16. 摆	bǎi	place
摆放	bǎifàng	arrange
17. 搞	gǎo	do
搞清楚	gǎo qīngchu	make clear
搞定	gǎodìng	work it
18. 指	zhǐ	point;finger
指出	zhǐchū	point out
手指	shǒuzhǐ	finger
19. 负	fù	bear
负责	fùzé	be responsible for
20. 争	zhēng	compete;argue
争取	zhēngqǔ	strive for
争论	zhēnglùn	debate

21.	流	liú	flow
	流利	liúlì	fluent
	交流	jiāoliú	exchange
	流行	liúxíng	prevail
22.	汤	tāng	soup
	喝汤	hē tāng	have soup
23.	数	①shù	number
	算数	suànshù	hold；stand
		②shǔ	count
	数一数二	shǔ yī shǔ èr	count as one of the best
24.	敌	dí	enemy
	敌人	dírén	enemy
25.	调	①diào	tune；move
	调查	diàochá	investigate
	声调	shēngdiào	tune
	语调	yǔdiào	tone
		②tiáo	suit well
	调整	tiáozhěng	adjust
26.	举	jǔ	lift
	举行	jǔxíng	hold（a meeting，etc.）
	举办	jǔbàn	conduct；hold
27.	育	yù	educate
	教育	jiàoyù	educate；education
	体育	tǐyù	physical education
28.	责	zé	duty；demand
	责任	zérèn	responsibility
29.	债	zhài	debt
	借债	jiè zhài	loan
30.	克	kè	gram；overcome
	克服	kèfú	overcome
	巧克力	qiǎokèlì	chocolate
31.	兑	duì	exchang；convert

	兑换	duìhuàn	exchange
32.	规	guī	regulation
	规定	guīdìng	stipulate
33.	联	lián	unite
	联系	liánxì	contact
	联欢	liánhuān	have a get-together
	联合	liánhé	unite;joint
	互联网	hùliánwǎng	internet
34.	章	zhāng	seal
	文章	wénzhāng	article
35.	虽	suī	although
	虽然	suīrán	although
36.	卡	①kǎ	card
	卡车	kǎchē	truck
	信用卡	xìnyòngkǎ	credit card
	卡拉OK	kǎlā'ōukèi	karaoke
		②qiǎ	get stuck;clip
	卡子	qiǎzi	pin
37.	乡	xiāng	village
	家乡	jiāxiāng	hometown

记忆窍门
Tips for Memorizing Work

一 形声字声旁记忆
Memorize the following characters with the given phonetic elements.

到 dào

（　）到 _____

（　）倒 fall　　倒下 dǎoxià　　fall down

		(丶)	倒	pour	倒茶	dào chá	pour tea

北 běi

(ˉ)	背	carry on one's back				
			背包	bēibāo	knapsack	
(丶)	背	back	背后	bèihòu	behind one's back	

考 kǎo

( )	考					
(ˇ)	烤	roast	烤鸭	kǎoyā	roast duck	
(ˇ)	拷	copy	拷贝	kǎobèi	copy	

董 dǒng

( )	懂					
(ˇ)	董	director	董事长	dǒngshìzhǎng	chairman of the board of directors	

太 tài

(丶)	态	status	态度	tàidu	attitude	

夫 fū

(ˉ)	肤	skin	皮肤	pífū	skin	
(ˊ)	扶	support with a hand				
			扶手	fúshǒu	handrail	

建 jiàn

( )	健					
(丶)	键	key	关键	guānjiàn	key	
			键盘	jiànpán	key board	
			关键词	guānjiàn cí	keyword	

马 mǎ

( )	吗					
( )	妈					
( )	码					
(ˇ)	玛		玛丽	Mǎlì	Mary	

（ˋ） 骂　curse　　骂人　mà rén　　　　swear at somebody

义　yì
　　（ˋ） 议　discuss　　会议　huìyì　　　meeting
　　　　　　　　　　　建议　jiànyì　　　suggest
　　　　　　　　　　　议论　yìlùn　　　discussion
　　（ˊ） 仪　instrument; ceremony
　　　　　　　　　　　仪器　yíqì　　　　instrument

介　jiè
　　（ ） 介 _____
　　（ˉ） 阶　stair　　阶段　jiēduàn　　stage
　　（jià） 价　cost　　价钱　jiàqián　　price
　　　　　　　　　　讨价还价　tǎo jià huán jià　　bargain

| 倒 | 背 | 烤 | 拷 | 董 | 态 | 肤 | 扶 | 键 | 玛 | 骂 | 议 | 仪 | 阶 | 价 |

二　形声字形旁记忆

Memorize the following characters with the given pictographic elements.

扌——摆　bǎi　　place　　　摆放　bǎifàng　　　arrange
　　搞　gǎo　　do　　　　搞清楚　gǎo qīngchu　make clear
　　　　　　　　　　　　搞定　gǎodìng　　　work it
　　指　zhǐ　　point; finger　指出　zhǐchū　　　point out
　　　　　　　　　　　　手指　shǒuzhǐ　　　finger

⺈——负　fù　　bear　　　　负责　fùzé　　　be responsible for
　　争　zhēng　compete; argue
　　　　　　　　　　　　争取　zhēngqǔ　　strive for
　　　　　　　　　　　　争论　zhēnglùn　　debate

氵——流　liú　　flow　　　　流利　liúlì　　　flow, fluent
　　　　　　　　　　　　交流　jiāoliú　　　exchange
　　　　　　　　　　　　流行　liúxíng　　　prevail

汤	tāng	soup	喝汤	hē tāng		have soup

攵——数	数	shù	number	算数	suàn shù	hold, stand
		shǔ	count	数一数二	shǔ yī shǔ èr	be count as one of the very best
	敌	dí	enemy	敌人	dírén	enemy

摆	搞	指	负	争	流	汤	数	敌

三 基本字带字

Memorize the following characters with the given basic elements.

周——调

周				
调	diào	调查	diàochá	investigate
		声调	shēngdiào	tune
		语调	yǔdiào	tone
调	tiáo	调整	tiáozhěng	adjust

兴——举

兴				
举	jǔ	举行	jǔxíng	hold(a meeting)
		举办	jǔbàn	conduct

云——运——育

云				
运				
育	yù	教育	jiàoyù	educate;education
		体育	tǐyù	physical education

责——绩——债

责	zé	责任	zérèn	responsibility
绩				
债	zhài	借债	jiè zhài	raise a loan

兄——克——兑

兄			
克	kè	克服　kèfú	overcome
		巧克力　qiǎokèlì	chocolate
兑	duì	兑换　duìhuàn	exchange

调	举	育	责	债	克	兑

四　部件构字

Memorize the following characters formed by the given parts.

夫 ╲
　　规　　guī　　　规定　guīdìng　　　stipulate
见 ╱

耳 ╲
　　联　　lián　　　联系　liánxì　　　contact
关 ╱　　　　　　　联欢　liánhuān　　have a get-together
　　　　　　　　　联合　liánhé　　　unite;joint
　　　　　　　　　互联网　hùliánwǎng　internet

立 ╲
　　章　　zhāng　　文章　wénzhāng　　article
早 ╱

口 ╲
　　虽　　suī　　　虽然　suīrán　　　althoug
虫 ╱

上 ╲
　　卡　　kǎ　　　卡车　kǎchē　　　truck
卜 ╱　　　　　　　信用卡　xìnyòngkǎ　credit card
　　　　　　　　　卡拉OK　kǎlā'ōukèi　karaoke

乡　　xiāng　　家乡　jiāxiāng　　hometown

规	联	章	虽	卡	乡

活用园地
Corner for Flexible Usage

 组词
Form words and phrases.

倒　①dǎo
　　打倒　over throw　病倒　fall ill
　　②dào
　　倒退　move backward　倒车　reverse a vehicle
　　倒数　count backward　倒影　inverted reflection in water
　　倒计时　countdown

背　①bēi
　　背起来　put something on one's back
　　背得动　strong enough to carry something on the back
　　背不动　not strong enough to carry something on the back
　　②bèi
　　背课文　recite the text　背书　learn the book by heart
　　背上　on the back　背面　backside　背心　a sleeveless garment
　　背景　back ground　背影　a view of someone's back
　　背光　stand in one's own light　背地里　on the sly
　　手背　back of the hand

烤　烤鸡　roast chicken　烤肉　roast meat

董　董事　director　董事会　board of directors　古董　curio

态　动态　trend　事态　situation　体态　physical form
　　表态　state one's stand on
　　一反常态　depart from one's normal behaviour

肤　皮肤病　skin disease　肤色　color of skin　肤浅　shallow

扶　扶助　assist　扶手　handrail

健　健康　health　健美　vigorous and graceful
　　健美操　bodybuilding exercise　健全　perfect　健谈　talkative

骂　叫骂　shout and curse　骂人话　curse　骂街　shout abuses in public

议　建议　suggest　提议　propose　商议　discuss

议会 parliament 议论 discussion 议员 parliament member
参议院 senate 不可思议 unthinkable

仪　仪式 ceremony 签字仪式 signing ceremony
介　介意 mind 介词 preposition 中介 go-between
阶　台阶 stair 阶层 stratum 阶级 class
价　物价 price 高价 high price 低价 low price
牌价 list price 比价 exchange rate 原价 orginal price
特价 special price 平价 normal price 半价 half price
还价 counter-offer 降价 reduce the prices

摆　摆动 wave 摆脱 get away from 摆架子 put on airs
搞　搞清楚 make clear 搞关系 establish relationship 搞笑 amuse
搞点儿吃的 get something to eat
指　指示 instruction；indicate 指引 guide
指点 show how（to do sth.） 指定 appoint 指令 instruction
指明 show clearly 指标 target 指手画脚 gesticulate
食指 index finger 中指 middle finger 无名指 ring finger
小指 little finger

负　胜负 victory or defeat 正负 positive or negative
争　争光 win glory for 争议 dispute 争气 try to bring credit to
力争 strive for 争先恐后 strive to be the first and fear to lag behind
流　河流 rivers 流动 flow 电流 electric current 气流 airflow
流水 flowing water 流通 circulate
汤　鸡汤 chicken soup 菜汤 vegetable soup 汤勺 ladle
数　①shǔ
数一数二 count as one of the very best
②shù
岁数 age 数目 number 数学 mathematics 数字 number
数词 numeral 多数 majority 少数 minority
概数 round number 总数 total number 次数 time
分数 mark 数码相机 digital camera
敌　敌意 hostility 情敌 rival in a love affair
调　①diào
调换 exchange 调动 transfer
调度 dispatch 色调 tone 单调 dull

②tiáo

调皮 naughty　调节 adjust　调料 seasoning
调和 reconciliation　调解 mediate
风调雨顺 good weather for the crops　空调 air conditioner

举 举动 movement　举止 manner　举重 weight lifting
检举 inform against　一举两得 kill two birds with one stone
举一反三 draw inferences about other cases from one instance
轻而易举 as easy as a piece of cake

育 发育 grow　生育 give birth to　体育场 stadium
体育馆 gymnasium

责 责任感 sense of responsibility　责备 reproach　责怪 blame
责骂 scold

债 还债 pay the debt　债务 debt　债主 creditor
负债 be in debt　欠债 be in debt　内债 internal debt
外债 external debt

克 一千克 a kilogram　休克 shock　巧克力 chocolate　马克 mark

兑 兑换率(lǜ) rate of exchange　兑换处 moneychanger　兑现 cash

规 规划 planning　规章 regulation　常规 regular rules
法规 regular　正规 statutes　家规 family rules
校规 school rules　圆规 compasses

联 联合 unite　联欢会 get-together　联想 associate
新闻联播 news hookup　联合国 the United Nations
对联 antithetical couplet　春联 Spring Festival couplets

章 报章 newspaper　简章 general regulations
规章 regulations and rules　违章 violation of the rules

卡 ①kǎ

卡片 card　卡路里 calorie　卡车 truck　借书卡 library card
贺年卡 New Year card　卡拉 OK karaoke

②qiǎ

发卡 hairpin　关卡 pass

乡 故乡 native place　乡村 village　乡亲 folks
城乡 town and country　思乡 miss one's home
同乡 a fellow villager, townsman or provincial

二 认读句子

Read and try to understand the following sentences.

1. 对不起，碰倒了你的车，我马上给你扶起来。

   I'm sorry I've knocked down your bike. I'll prop it up immediately.

2. 你的背包挂在门背后了。

   Your bag hangs at the back of the door.

3. 服务员，请给我倒杯茶。

   Waiter, pour me a cup of tea, please.

4. 董事长来了，会议可以开始了。

   Now that the chairman is here, let's begin our meeting.

5. 他对人很热情，态度很好。

   He is kind to others.

6. 同志，我想挂个号，挂皮肤科。

   Hello, I would like to register at the dermatological department.

7. 请抓好扶手，汽车要拐弯了。

   Please hold on to the rail. The bus is turning a corner.

8. 玛丽去健身房锻炼了。

   Mary has gone to the gymnasium.

9. 我现在关键的问题是汉字，我觉得汉字很难。

   Now the key problem for me is learning to write Chinese characters. I find it very difficult to do it.

10. 这种仪器价钱很贵。

    This instrument is very expensive.

11. 在汉语学习的初级阶段，语音语调和声调特别重要。

    At the beginning stage of learning Chinese, pronunciation, intonation and tone are particularly important.

12. 今天晚上的生日晚会，我负责买水果，你负责做菜。

    I'm to buy fruits and you're to do the cooking for the birthday party tonight.

13. 这个文章介绍了北京烤鸭的历史，你想不想看看？

    This article tells about the history of Peking roast duck. Would you like to read it?

14. 他汉语说得很流利。

    He speaks fluent Chinese.

15. 我们先出去散会儿步，回来以后再喝汤。
Let's go for a walk first and have the soup after it.

16. 敌人的卡车开过来了。
The enemy's truck is coming over.

17. 下星期我们要调整一下课表。
We'll have to adjust the timetable next week.

18. 去年，我们学校举行了一次网球比赛，他哥哥得了第一名。
We held a tennis match in our school last year, and his brother won the first prize.

19. 张老师的孩子体育成绩不太好。
Instructor Zhang's child doesn't do well in physical education.

20. 为了给他爸爸治病，他们家借了不少债。
They have borrowed a lot of money in order to cure his father.

21. 他妈妈规定他晚上十点以前必须回家。
His mother demands that he come back before 10 o'clock pm.

22. 100 美元兑换 827 元人民币，请你数一数。
You have 827 *yuan* RMB for your 100 US dollars.

23. 王老师，你给我留个电话号码吧，回国以后我好跟你联系。
Instructor Wang, please give me your phone number so that I can contact you after I'm back to my country.

24. 我很想念我的家乡。
I miss my hometown very much.

25. 我们一定要克服困难，争取取得好的成绩。
We must overcome the difficulty and strive for good results.

26. 给病人治病，这是医生应负的责任，你不用客气。
Not at all. It is the doctor's responsibility to cure the patient.

27. 不用卡子卡住就会散开来，你去找个卡子来。
It will fall into pieces without a pin. Go and get a pin.

28. 这些都是名牌货，所以价钱比较贵。
These are all famous-brand products. So their prices are very high.

29. 这件事还没有搞清楚，现在还不知道主要是谁的责任。
The matter has not been clear yet and no one knows whom the main responsibility lies with.

30. 她总是把家里的东西摆放得整整齐齐的。
She always puts everything in her house in good order

31. 我的汉语说得不太好，说错的地方请你及时给我指出来，好吗？
My oral Chinese is not so good. While I'm speaking, please point out my mistakes promptly, OK?

自学园地

Corner for Self-study

一 给下列词语注音

Mark the following words with phonetic symbols.

调整	联系	负责	态度	关键
( )	( )	( )	( )	( )
调查	举行	争取	议论	规定
( )	( )	( )	( )	( )

二 写出本课含有下列偏旁的汉字并注音

Write out the characters with the following elements in this lesson, and mark them with phonetic symbols.

月：_____（　　　）　　_____（　　　）　　_____（　　　）

扌：_____（　　　）　　_____（　　　）　　_____（　　　）　　_____（　　　）

亻：_____（　　　）　　_____（　　　）　　_____（　　　）　　_____（　　　）

⻊：_____（　　　）　　_____（　　　）

讠：_____（　　　）　　_____（　　　）

攵：_____（　　　）　　_____（　　　）

三 在括号内加上合适的词语

Fill in the blanks with right words and phrases.

（　　　）的态度　　　（　　　）的文章　　　（　　　）的家乡

（　　　）的责任　　　（　　　）的建议　　　（　　　）的规定

（　　　）的价钱　　　（　　　）的手指　　　（　　　）的仪器

调查（　　　）　　　举行（　　　）　　　指出（　　　）

争论（　　　）　　　交流（　　　）　　　克服（　　　）

兑换（　　　）　　　调整（　　　）　　　教育（　　　）

四 给下列多音字注音并组词

Mark the following polyphones with phonetic symbols, and form words and phrases with them.

背 ⟨（　　）＿＿＿＿＿
　　⟨（　　）＿＿＿＿＿

数 ⟨（　　）＿＿＿＿＿
　　⟨（　　）＿＿＿＿＿

倒 ⟨（　　）＿＿＿＿＿
　　⟨（　　）＿＿＿＿＿

调 ⟨（　　）＿＿＿＿＿
　　⟨（　　）＿＿＿＿＿

卡 ⟨（　　）＿＿＿＿＿
　　⟨（　　）＿＿＿＿＿

五 阅读下列句子并回答问题

Read the following sentences and answer the questions accordingly.

1. 市长在昨天的物价工作会议上指出：降低物价是今年工作中最关键的问题。

   昨天的会议主要讨论了什么问题？

2. 这些仪器虽然都是进口的，价钱很贵，但也常常会出问题。

   这些仪器怎么样？

3. 下星期王教授要出国参加一个学术交流会议，所以下周你们举行的联欢会他参加不了了。

   王教授为什么不来参加下周的联欢会？

4. 学校、家庭、社会应该联合起来，共同负起教育孩子的责任，这样，才能让我们的孩子健康快乐地成长。

   孩子们怎么样才能健康成长？

5. 我们班数董小刚个子最高，他不但学习成绩好，而且体育成绩在班里也是数一数二的。

   董小刚个子怎么样？

6. 这些东西你都可以上互联网查找，你只需在键盘上键入关键词，电脑几秒（miǎo, second）钟就可以搞定，电脑上显示出来的东西，哪些是你需要的，你只要拷贝下来就可以了。

   这些东西在网上怎么样？

7. 他在上次<u>举办</u>的"外国人唱中文歌"大赛上得了第二名,那些中文的<u>流行</u>歌曲,都是他跟朋友去唱<u>卡拉</u>OK 时学会的。

"他"参加了什么比赛? 是怎么学会那些中文歌的?

8. 有的报纸说,吃<u>巧克力</u>对身体不好,会发胖,<u>然而</u>昨天我在报纸上看到的<u>文章</u>说,吃<u>巧克力</u>对人的身体有好处,我<u>搞不清楚</u>,我们到底应该听谁的?

什么问题搞不清楚?

第七课

汉字园地
Corner for Chinese Characters

1.	抓	zhuā	get hold of arrest
	抓紧	zhuājǐn	seize
2.	未	wèi	not yet
	未来	wèilái	future
	未必	wèibì	may not
3.	味	wèi	taste
	味道	wèidào	flavor
4.	吴	Wú	a surname
5.	误	wù	mistake
	错误	cuòwù	error
	误会	wùhuì	misunderstand
6.	响	xiǎng	sound; loud
	影响	yǐngxiǎng	influence
	响应	xiǎngyìng	respond
7.	按	àn	press; according to
	按照	ànzhào	according to
	按时	ànshí	on time
8.	案	àn	(law) case
	答案	dá'àn	answer
	方案	fāng'àn	scheme
9.	胜	shèng	win

胜利	shènglì	victory
名胜	míngshèng	scenic spot
10. 像	xiàng	photo
好像	hǎoxiàng	look like
画像	huàxiàng	portrait
11. 橡	xiàng	oak; rubber tree
橡皮	xiàngpí	rubber
12. 乘	chéng	take (a means of transport)
乘客	chéngkè	passenger
13. 剩	shèng	surplus
剩下	shèngxià	be left
过剩	guòshèng	excess; surplus
14. 李	Lǐ	a surname
李子	lǐzi	plum
15. 晒	shài	dry in the sun
晒衣服	shài yīfu	dry clothes in the sun
16. 洒	sǎ	spray
洒水	sǎ shuǐ	spray water
17. 温	wēn	warm
气温	qìwēn	temperature
温暖	wēnnuǎn	warm
18. 湿	shī	moist
湿度	shīdù	moisture
19. 命	mìng	order; fate; life
命运	mìngyùn	fate; destiny
生命	shēngmìng	life
20. 伞	sǎn	umbrella
雨伞	yǔsǎn	umbrella
21. 择	zé	pick
选择	xuǎnzé	choice
择业	zé yè	select a job
22. 释	shì	interpret
解释	jiěshì	explain

23.	激	jī	excite; stimulate
	激动	jīdòng	excited
	感激	gǎnjī	gratitude
	激光	jīguāng	laser
24.	邀	yāo	invite
	邀请	yāoqǐng	invitation
25.	愉	yú	pleased
	愉快	yúkuài	happy
26.	掌	zhǎng	palm; paw; be in charge of
	掌握	zhǎngwò	master; control
	掌上电脑	zhǎngshàng diànnǎo	palmtop
27.	仅	jǐn	only
	不仅	bùjǐn	not only
28.	叹	tàn	sigh
	叹气	tàn qì	give a sigh
29.	权	quán	power
	权力	quánlì	power
	权利	quánlì	right
30.	选	xuǎn	select
	选举	xuǎnjǔ	elect; election
31.	几	jī	table
	茶几	chájī	tea table
32.	了	liǎo	(used after a verb plus 得 or 不) to a finish; end; know
	了不起	liǎobuqǐ	terrific; marve lous
	不得了	bùdéliǎo	extremely
33.	为	wéi	for; by; be
	认为	rènwéi	think
	以为	yǐwéi	think
	成为	chéngwéi	become

34.	发	fà	hair
	头发	tóufa	hair
35.	重	chóng	repeat
	重复	chóngfù	repetition
	重新	chóngxīn	again
36.	的	①dí	true; really
	的确	díquè	indeed
		②dì	purpose
	目的	mùdì	purpose
37.	种	zhòng	grow; plant
	种花	zhòng huā	grow flowers
38.	应	①yīng	should
	应当	yīngdāng	should
		②yìng	answer; promise; deal with
	应用	yìngyòng	apply
	答应	dāying	answer; agree
	反应	fǎnyìng	respond; response
	应邀	yìngyāo	at the invitation

记忆窍门
Tips for Memorizing Work

一 形声字声旁记忆

Memorize the following characters with the given phonetic elements.

爪　zhuǎ

（一）抓　get hold of　　抓紧　zhuājǐn　　seize

未　wèi

（丶）未　not yet　　未来　wèilái　　future
　　　　　　　　　未必　wèibì　　may not

（ ` ）	味	taste	味道	wèidào	flavor

吴 Wú

（ ´ ）	吴	a surname			
（ ` ）	误	mistake	错误	cuòwù	error
			误会	wùhuì	misunderstand

向 xiàng

（ ）	向	_____			
（ ˇ ）	响	sound; loud	影响	yǐngxiǎng	influence
			响应	xiǎngyìng	respond

安 ān

（ ` ）	按	press	按照	ànzhào	according to
			按时	ànshí	on time
（ ` ）	案	case	答案	dá'àn	answer
			方案	fāng'àn	scheme

生 shēng

（ ` ）	胜	win	胜利	shènglì	victory
			名胜	míngshèng	scenic spot
（ ）	姓	_____			
（ ）	星	_____			

象 xiàng

（ ）	象	_____			
（ ` ）	像	photo; resemble	好像	hǎoxiàng	look like
			画像	huàxiàng	portrait
（ ` ）	橡	oak; rubber tree	橡皮	xiàngpí	rubber

乘 chéng

（ ´ ）	乘	take (a means of transport)			
			乘客	chéngkè	passenger
(shèng)	剩	surplus	剩下	shèngxià	be left
			过剩	guòshèng	excess; surplus

抓	未	味	吴	误	响	按	案	胜	像	橡	乘	剩

二　比较下列形近字

Compare the following characters with similar pictographic elements.

李——季

| 李 | Lǐ | a surname | 李子 | lǐzi | plum |
| 季 | | | | | |

晒——洒

| 晒 | shài | dry in the sun | 晒衣服 | shài yīfu | dry clothes in the sun |
| 洒 | sǎ | spray | 洒水 | sǎ shuǐ | spray water |

温——湿

温	wēn	warm	气温	qìwēn	temperature
			温暖	wēnnuǎn	warm
湿	shī	moist	湿度	shīdù	moisture

命——伞

命	mìng	order；fate	生命	shēngmìng	life
			命运	mìngyùn	fate
伞	sǎn	umbrella	雨伞	yǔsǎn	umbrella

择——释

择	zé	pick	选择	xuǎnzé	choice
			择业	zé yè	select a job
释	shì	interpret	解释	jiěshì	explain

激——邀

激	jī	excite	激动	jīdòng	excited
			感激	gǎnjī	gratitude
			激光	jīguāng	laser
邀	yāo	invite	邀请	yāoqǐng	invitation

输——偷——愉

输					
偷					
愉	yú	pleased	愉快	yúkuài	happy

常——掌

常		
掌	zhǎng	palm; paw; be in charge of
	掌握	zhǎngwò master; control

仅——叹——权

仅	jǐn	only	不仅	bùjǐn	not only
叹	tàn	sigh	叹气	tàn qì	give a sigh
权	quán	power	权力	quánlì	power

选——洗

| 选 | xuǎn | select | 选举 | xuǎnjǔ | elect |
| 洗 | | | | | |

| 李 | 晒 | 洒 | 温 | 湿 | 命 | 伞 | 择 | 释 | 激 | 邀 | 愉 | 掌 | 仅 |

| 叹 | 权 | 选 |

三 比较下列多音字

Compare the following polyphones.

几	jǐ			
	jī	茶几	chájī	tea table
了	le			
	liǎo	不得了	bùdéliǎo	extremely
为	wèi			
	wéi	认为	rènwéi	think
		以为	yǐwéi	think
		成为	chéngwéi	become
发	fā			
	fà	头发	tóufa	hair
重	zhòng			
	chóng	重复	chóngfù	repetition
		重新	chóngxīn	again

的	de			
	dí	的确	díquè	indeed
	dì	目的	mùdì	purpose
种	zhǒng			
	zhòng	种花	zhòng huā	grow flowers
应	yīng			
		应当	yīngdāng	should
	yìng	应用	yìngyòng	apply
		答应	dāying	answer；agree
		反应	fǎnyìng	respond；response
		应邀	yìngyāo	at the invitation

几	了	为	发	重	的	种	应

活用园地

Corner for Flexible Usage

 一 组词

Form words and phrases.

抓   抓住 seize 抓起来 arrest 抓阄(jiū)儿 draw lots

未   未必 not necessarily 未婚 unmarried 未婚夫 fiancé
      未婚妻 fiancée 未知数 uncertain 前所未有 unprecedented

味   香味 fragrance 臭味 odor 酒味 alcoholic flavor
      药味 medicine flavor 美味 delicious 气味 smell
      口味 taste 调味 seasoning 野味 game 风味 flavor
      味精 MSG 味觉 sense of taste

误   误差 error 误会 misunderstand 误解 misread
      误火车 miss the train 误飞机 miss the plane 失误 error

响   响应 respond 响亮 loud and clear 响声 sound 音响 acoustics

按   按期 on time 按说 normally；ordinarily

案	教案 teaching plan	报案 report a criminal case
	作案 commit a crime 破案 solve a case 提案 motion
	案件 case 案情 details of a case

胜	胜负 victory or defeat 胜任 competent 取胜 win victory
	好胜 love to outshine others 胜地 a famous scenic spot
	名胜 scenic spot 不可胜数 innumerable

| 象 | 气象 meteorology 对象 object 现象 phenomenon |
| | 想象 imagine 象棋 chess 象牙 ivory |

| 像 | 人像 portrait 石像 stone statue 头像 head portrait or sculpture |
| | 图像 image 像样 presentable 不像话 indecent |

| 橡 | 橡树 oak |

乘	乘凉 cool oneself in the shade 乘车 take a bus
	乘船 by boat 乘飞机 by air 乘务员 conductor
	乘机 seize the opportunity

| 剩 | 剩余 surplus 剩下 be left |

| 洒 | 洒香水 spray perfume |

| 晒 | 晒台 balcony 晒太阳 have a sun bath 晒衣服 dry clothes in the sun |

温	温差 temperature difference 温暖 warm 温泉 hot spring
	温带 temperate zone 高温 high temperature
	低温 low temperature 体温 body temperature
	温室 greenhouse 降温 lower the temperature
	温和 mild 温度计 thermometer

| 湿 | 湿气 moisture |

命	命令 order 生命力 vitality 革命 revolution
	拼命 exert oneself regardless of danger to one's life 使命 mission
	玩命 risk one's life 算命 fortune-telling 要命 extremely
	命名 name 命题 assign a topic

| 伞 | 一把伞 an umbrella 打伞 hold up an umbrella |

| 释 | 注释 note 释放 release 爱不释手 be so fond of something that one will not let it out of one's hand |

| 激 | 激发 stimulate 激光 laser 激情 passion 感激 gratitude |

| 邀 | 邀请赛 invitational tournament 特邀 specially invite |

| 掌 | 手掌 palm 掌声 applause 掌权 be in power |

| 权 | 人权 human rights 主权 sovereignty 特权 privilege |

叹　　感叹　exclaim　叹词　exclamatory

选　　选出　elect　选票　vote　选民　voter　选取　choose
　　　选手　contestant　选用　select and employ　选派　select and send
　　　入选　be selected　当选　be elected　评选　assess and select

几　　几乎　almost　窗明几净　with bright windows and clean tables

了　　了结　conclude　明了　understand　办得了　can be done
　　　办不了　cannot be done　受得了　can stand
　　　受不了　cannot stand　没完没了　endless

为　　①wèi
　　　为了　for　为什么　why　因为　because
　　　②wéi
　　　作为　conduct；as　行为　behavior　人为　man-made
　　　为首　headed by　为止　till　为难　make things difficult for
　　　为期　by a definite date　习以为常　be used to sth.
　　　自以为是　cocksure　不足为奇　nothing strange　一言为定　settled

发　　①fā
　　　发生　happen　发现　discover；discovery
　　　发展　develop；development　发烧　have a fever　发表　publish
　　　发出　give out　发达　developed　发动　start
　　　发明　invent；invention　发言　speak　发扬　develop
　　　发电　generate electricity　发火　get angry　发票　receipt
　　　发音　pronunciation　发育　grow
　　　②fà
　　　假发　artificial hair　发卡　hair pin　发式　hairstyle
　　　白发　gray hair

重　　①zhòng
　　　重要　important　重视　attach importance to
　　　重点　focal point　重大　significant　重量　weight
　　　重心　center of gravity　重工业　heavy industry
　　　②chóng
　　　重演　recur　重写　write again　重念　read again
　　　重唱　an ensemble of two or more singers，each singing one part
　　　重婚　bigamy

种　　①zhǒng
　　　种子　seed　种族　race　黄种人　the yellow race　种种　all sorts of

②zhòng

种菜　grow vegetables　种树　plant trees
种地　do farm work　种田　do farm work

二 认读句子

Read and try to understand the following sentences.

1. 我们快走吧，<u>抓紧</u>时间，别误了飞机。
   Hurry up, or else we'll miss the plane.

2. 北京的<u>名胜</u>我几乎都游览过，最喜欢的还是故宫。
   I have visited almost all the scenic spots in Beijing, of which I like the Palace Museum best.

3. 18 岁以上的人才有<u>选举权</u>。
   Persons of 18 and above have the right to vote.

4. 这道题只有两个<u>答案</u>，或者 A，或者 B，你<u>选择</u>哪一个？
   You have two choices to answer the question. Which would you choose, A or B?

5. 这是我爷爷年轻时候的<u>画像</u>。
   This is a portrait of my grandpa as a young man.

6. 可以借你的<u>橡皮</u>用一下吗？
   Can I use your eraser?

7. 我今天没带<u>雨伞</u>，下雨的时候，全身都<u>湿</u>了。
   I forgot to take the umbrella with me, and I was caught in the rain and drenched.

8. 那位<u>乘客</u>好像已经睡着了。
   The passenger seems to have fallen asleep.

9. 天气预报说，<u>未来</u>几天<u>气温</u>都很低。
   The weather forecast says that temperatures will be rather low in a couple of days.

10. 他在<u>阳台</u>上晒衣服呢。
    He's drying his clothes in the sun on the balcony.

11. 北京的冬天屋子里太干了，每天睡觉以前可以在<u>地上洒</u>点<u>水</u>。
    It is very dry inside the house in Beijing in winter. You had better spread some water on the floor before going to bed every day.

12. 看到自己的球队**胜**利了，他们**激动**得<u>不得了</u>。

They were very excited at the victory of their soccer team.

13. 李老师，我们大使馆今天晚上有一个晚会，可以<u>邀请</u>你参加吗？

Professor Li, we'd like to invite you to a party at our embassy tonight. Could you come?

14. 他<u>不仅</u>是我的老师，而且也是我最好的朋友。

He is my friend as well as my teacher.

15. 老吴，你怎么总是在<u>叹气</u>啊？

Mr. Wu, why do you keep sighing?

16. 他的<u>权力</u>很大。

He is a man of great power.

17. 父母不能总是<u>命令</u>孩子做什么。

Parents are not supposed to order their children about.

18. 沙发前面有一张<u>茶几</u>。

There is a tea table in front of the sofa.

19. <u>按照</u>那个航空公司的<u>规定</u>，飞机误点了，<u>乘客</u>有<u>权利</u>提出退票。

In accordance with the stipulation of the airline company, the passenger has the right to ask to return the ticket if the plane is late.

20. 老师，你刚才的<u>解释</u>我没听懂，你再<u>重复</u>一遍可以吗？

Professor, I failed to understand your explanation. Could you repeat it?

21. A：这个菜的<u>味道</u>怎么样？

What do you think of the taste of the dish?

B：味道<u>的确</u>不错！

It's delicious!

22. 我这次来中国的主要<u>目</u>的是学习汉语。

The purpose of this visit of mine to China is to study Chinese.

23. 我父母都是老师，受家庭的<u>影响</u>，大学毕业后我也<u>成为</u>了一名教师。

My parents are both teachers. Influenced by the family, I also became a teacher after graduation from college.

24. 只<u>剩</u>两个面包了，我们一人一个吧。

We have only two loaves of bread. Let's have one each.

25. 昨天你为什么迟到，能<u>解释</u>一下吗？

Can you explain why you were late yesterday?

26. 这个地方<u>湿度</u>比较低。

The place has a low moisture.

27. 我<u>按时</u>完成了学习任务。
    I finished my studies on time.

28. 这把<u>雨伞</u>多少钱？
    How much does the umbrella cost?

29. 这是他的<u>未婚妻</u>，姓<u>李</u>，是一名<u>了不起</u>的乒乓球运动员。
    This is his fiancée, Miss Li, a great table tennis ployer.

30. 他退休以后每天<u>养养鸟</u>、<u>种种花</u>，过得很愉快。
    After retirement, he keeps pet birds and grows flowers every day, having a good time.

自学园地

Corner for Self-study

一　给下列词语注音

Mark the following words with phonetic symbols.

影响	重复	激动	愉快	胜利
(　)	(　)	(　)	(　)	(　)

选择	解释	味道	按照	邀请
(　)	(　)	(　)	(　)	(　)

二　写出本课含有下列偏旁的汉字并注音

Write out the characters with the following elements in this lesson, and mark them with phonetic symbols.

扌：_____（　）　　_____（　）　　_____（　）

口：_____（　）　　_____（　）　　_____（　）

犭：_____（　）　　_____（　）　　_____（　）

木：_____（　）　　_____（　）　　_____（　）

辶：_____（　）　　_____（　）　　_____（　）

三 给下列多音字注音并组词

Mark the following polyphones with phonetic symbols, and form words and phrases with them.

几（　　）_____　　　的（　　）_____　　　种（　　）_____
（　　）_____　　　（　　）_____　　　（　　）_____

重（　　）_____　　　为（　　）_____　　　了（　　）_____
（　　）_____　　　（　　）_____　　　（　　）_____

四 在括号内加上合适的词语

Fill in the blanks with right words and phrases.

抓紧（　　　　）　按照（　　　　）　掌握（　　　　）　解释（　　　　）

选择（　　　　）　邀请（　　　　）　响应（　　　　）　答应（　　　　）

（　　　　）的头发　　　　（　　　　）的命运　　　　（　　　　）的乘客

（　　　　）的影响　　　　（　　　　）的名胜　　　　（　　　　）的方案

五 阅读下列句子并回答问题

Read the following sentences and answer the questions accordingly.

1. 昆明这个城市一年四季温暖如春，所以也叫做"春城"。
   为什么"昆明"被称为"春城"？

2. 这一次的发展方案关系到公司今后的命运，所以希望大家抓紧时间，好好研究，按时完成。
   这个方案重要不重要？

3. "你的医术真了不起，是你给了我女儿重新开始生活的机会。"老人握着李大夫的手，感激得流下了眼泪。
   老人为什么会向李大夫表示感激？

4. 你的确是误会他了。你以为他早就知道这件事，其实他也是今天刚知道的。
   "你"认为"他"知道不知道这件事？

5. 从练习中出现的这些错误可以看出，昨天学的语法，你还没有完全掌握。

说话人怎么知道他还没完全掌握昨天的语法？

6. 你这种病，现在应用激光技术完全可以治好，你放心好了。

"你"的病好治吗？

7. 生命对于人来说，只有一次，我们应当好好爱惜才好。未婚夫跟你分手，为了这么点事儿就想死吗？其实，结婚以前分手未必不是一件好事。

她为什么想死？

8. 今天我走在路上，对面走过来一个人，跟我打招呼："张老师，您好，您还记得我吗？"我答应了一声，还跟他聊了几句，但是当时没反应过来，只觉得他很面熟，却想不起来是谁。后来回到家才想起来，他是我五年以前的美国学生。

张老师还认识这个学生吗？

9. 我国国家主席（zhǔxí，president）应日本首相的邀请已于今日上午乘专机到达日本首都东京，开始了对日本为期三天的访问。

请给这条新闻加一个标题（biāotí，title），字数在十以内。

第八课

汉字园地
Corner for Chinese Characters

1.	诚	chéng	honest
	诚实	chéngshí	honesty
2.	趣	qù	interesting
	兴趣	xìngqù	interest
	感兴趣	gǎn xìngqù	take interest in
3.	郊	jiāo	suburban
	郊区	jiāoqū	suburbs
4.	华	huá	Chinese; brilliant
	中华	Zhōnghuá	China
5.	乔	Qiáo	a surname
	乔木	qiáomù	arbor
6.	侨	qiáo	expatriate
	华侨	huáqiáo	overseas Chinese
7.	紫	zǐ	purple
	紫色	zǐsè	purple
8.	烟	yān	cigarette; smoke; mist
	抽烟	chōu yān	smoke
9.	篇	piān	a measure word for paper, book leaves, articles, etc.
	一篇小说	yì piān xiǎoshuō	a novel

10.	偏	piān	slant;contrary to what is expected
	偏见	piānjiàn	prejudice
11.	骗	piàn	cheat
	受骗	shòu piàn	be cheated
12.	毯	tǎn	carpet
	毯子	tǎnzi	blanket
	地毯	dìtǎn	floor carpet
13.	连	lián	link;in succession
	连忙	liánmáng	hurriedly
	连……都/也	lián···dōu/yě	even
	连续	liánxù	continuously
14.	追	zhuī	run after
	追求	zhuīqiú	pursuit
	追星族	zhuīxīngzú	star fan
15.	迹	jì	trace
	名胜古迹	míngshèng gǔjì	scenic spots and historical sites
16.	造	zào	make
	造句	zào jù	make sentences
	改造	gǎizào	transform
17.	划	①huá	row
	划船	huá chuán	row a boat
		②huà	plan
	计划	jìhuà	plan
18.	刷	shuā	brush;eliminate
	刷牙	shuā yá	clean one's teeth
	刷卡	shuā kǎ	punch the card
19.	制	zhì	make;system
	制造	zhìzào	manufacture
	制度	zhìdù	system
	AA制	ēi-ēi zhì	go Dutch
20.	创	chuàng	establish;start

创造	chuàngzào	create
创作	chuàngzuò	create; creation
21. 节	jié	festival; save
节日	jiérì	holiday
节目	jiémù	program
春节	Chūn Jié	the Spring Festival
国庆节	Guóqìng Jié	National Day
中秋节	Zhōngqiū Jié	Mid-autumn Festival
节约	jiéyuē	economize
季节	jìjié	season
22. 营	yíng	operate; camp
营业	yíngyè	do business
营养	yíngyǎng	nutrition
23. 糟	zāo	poor
糟糕	zāogāo	too bad
24. 糕	gāo	cake
蛋糕	dàngāo	cake
25. 抽	chōu	take out from in between; draw
抽象	chōuxiàng	abstract
26. 掉	diào	fall
掉眼泪	diào yǎnlèi	shed tears
27. 社	shè	society; organized body
社会	shèhuì	society
旅行社	lǚxíngshè	travel agency
社区	shèqū	community
28. 神	shén	god; spirit; magical
精神	jīngshén	spirit
29. 却	què	step back; but
退却	tuìquè	retreat
30. 既	jì	since, both... (and)
既然	jìrán	now that
既……也……	jì...yě	both... and
既……又……	jì...yòu	as well as

31. 册	cè	volume
手册	shǒucè	manual
32. 诞	dàn	birth
圣诞节	Shèngdàn Jié	Christmas
33. 圣	shèng	saint
圣经	Shèngjīng	the Bible
34. 横	héng	horizontal
人行横道	rénxíng héngdào	zebra crossing
35. 另	lìng	other; another
另外	lìngwài	besides
36. 拐	guǎi	turn
往右拐	wǎng yòu guǎi	turn right
37. 引	yǐn	draw
引起	yǐnqǐ	cause
吸引	xīyǐn	attract
38. 乱	luàn	disorder
乱糟糟	luànzāozāo	messy
乱七八糟	luàn qī bā zāo	in a mess; in terrible disorder

记忆窍门
Tips for Memorizing Work

一 形声字声旁记忆

Memorize the following characters with the given phonetic elements.

成　　chéng

（ ）城 _____

（ˊ）诚　honest　　　　诚实 chéngshí　　　honesty

取　qǔ
（ ）取 _____
（ˋ）趣　interesting　兴趣　xìngqù　interest
　　　　　　　　　　　感兴趣　gǎn xìngqù　take interest in

交　jiāo
（ ）饺 _____
（ ）较 _____
（一）郊　suburban　郊区　jiāoqū　suburbs

化　huà
（ ）化 _____
（ˊ）华　Chinese　中华　Zhōnghuá　China

乔　qiáo
（ ）桥 _____
（ˊ）乔　disguise　乔木　qiáomù　arbor
（ˊ）侨　expatriate　华侨　huáqiáo　overseas Chinese

此　cǐ
（zǐ）紫　purple　紫色　zǐsè　purple

因　yīn
（ ）因 _____
（yān）烟　cigarette　抽烟　chōu yān　smoke

诚	趣	郊	华	乔	侨	紫	烟

二　比较下列形近字

Compare the following characters with similar pictographic elements.

篇——偏——骗

篇　a measure word for paper,book leaves,articles,etc.
　　一篇小说　yì piān xiǎoshuō　a novel

| 偏 | partial | 偏见 | piānjiàn | prejudice |
| 骗 | cheat | 受骗 | shòu piàn | be cheated |

谈——毯

谈				
毯	carpet	毯子	tǎnzi	blanket
		地毯	dìtǎn	carpet

| 篇 | 偏 | 骗 | 毯 |

三 形声字形旁记忆

Memorize the following characters with the given pictographic elements.

辶——连	lián	link	连忙	liánmáng	hurriedly
			连……都/也	lián…dōu/yě	even
			连续	liánxù	continuously
追	zhuī	run after	追求	zhuīqiú	pursuit
			追星族	zhuīxīngzú	star fan
迹	jì	trace	名胜古迹	míngshèng gǔjì	scenic spots and historical sites
造	zào	make	造句	zào jù	make sentences
			改造	gǎizào	transform
刂——划	①huá	row	划船	huá chuán	row a boat
	②huà	plan	计划	jìhuà	plan
刷	shuā	brush	刷牙	shuā yá	clean one's teeth
			刷卡	shuā kǎ	punch the card
制	zhì	make;system	制造	zhìzào	create
			制度	zhìdù	system
			AA制	ēi-ēi zhì	go Dutch
创	chuàng	establish	创造	chuàngzào	create
			创作	chuàngzuò	create;creation
⺾——节	jié	festival;save	节日	jiérì	holiday
			节目	jiémù	program

			春节	Chūn Jié	the Spring Festival	
			国庆节	Guóqìng Jié	National Day	
			中秋节	Zhōngqiū Jié	the Mid-autumn Festival	
			节约	jiéyuē	economize	
			季节	jìjié	season	
营	yíng	operate	营业	yíngyè	do business	
			营养	yíngyǎng	nutrition	
米——糟	zāo	poor	糟糕	zāogāo	too bad	
糕	gāo	cake	蛋糕	dàngāo	cake	
扌——抽	chōu	draw	抽象	chōuxiàng	abstract	
掉	diào	fall	掉眼泪	diào yǎnlèi	shed tears	
礻——社	shè	society	社会	shèhuì	society	
			旅行社	lǚxíngshè	travel agency	
			社区	shèqū	community	
神	shén	spirit	精神	jīngshén	spirit	

连	追	迹	造	划	刷	制	创	节	营	糟	糕	抽	掉
社	神												

四　基本字带字

Memorize the following characters with the given basic elements.

却——脚

却	què	step back	退却	tuìquè		retreat
脚						

既——概

既	jì	since	既然	jìrán	now that
			既……也	jì…yě	both... and
			既……又	jì…yòu	as well as

概 _____

册——删

册　cè　volume　　手册　shǒucè　　manual

删 _____

延——诞

延 _____

诞　dàn　birth　　圣诞节　Shèngdàn Jié　　Christmas Day

圣——怪

圣　shèng　holy　　圣经　Shèngjīng　　the Holy Bible

怪 _____

黄——横

黄 _____

横　héng　horizontal　　人行横道　rénxíng héngdào　　zebra crossing

另——拐

另　lìng　other　　另外　lìngwài　　besides

拐　guǎi　turn　　往右拐　wǎng yòu guǎi　　turn right

弓——引

弓 _____

引　yǐn　draw　　引起　yǐnqǐ　　cause

　　　　　　　　吸引　xīyǐn　　attract

舌——乱

舌 _____

乱　luàn　disorder　　乱糟糟　luànzāozāo　　messy

　　　　　　　　乱七八糟　luàn qī bā zāo　　in a mess；in terrible disorder

却 既 册 诞 圣 横 另 拐 引 乱

活用园地
Corner for Flexible Usage

 组词
Form words and phrases.

诚	诚意 sincerity　热诚 enthusiasm　真诚 sincere 真心诚意 sincerity
趣	趣事 an interesting episode　趣味 interest　乐趣 fun 兴趣 interest 有趣 interesting　风趣 humorous
郊	郊外 outskirts　郊游 outing　近郊 suburbs 远郊 the outer suburbs
华	华贵 luxurious　华夏 China　华东 East China 华中 Central China　华北 North China　华南 South China 才华 talent　华人 Chinese　华裔(yì) foreign citizen of Chinese origin
侨	侨民 expatriate　侨居 expatriation
紫	紫红色 purple　青紫色 dark blue　紫菜 laver 万紫千红 extremely colorful
烟	烟草 tobacco　烟灰 cigarette ash
篇	一篇文章 an article　一篇课文 a text　长篇 a long text 短篇 a short text　中篇 a medium length of text　篇章 writings
偏	偏爱 bias　偏向 erroneous tendency　偏差 deviation 偏偏 deliberately　偏心 partial　偏旁 radical
骗	骗人 cheating　骗子 cheat
毯	毯子 blanket　毛毯 wool blanket　挂毯 wall blanket
连	连接 connect　连同 together with　连词 conjunction 接连 successively　连连 repeatedly　连年 successive years 连夜 all through the night　一连 continuously 接二连三 one after another
追	追上 catch up with　追查 trace　追究 find out 追问 question closely

迹	足迹 footprint 字迹 handwriting 事迹 deeds 奇迹 miracle	
	手迹 somebody's original handwriting or painting	
	笔迹 handwriting 迹象 sign	
造	建造 construct 改造 transform 制造 manufacture	
	人造 man-made 造反 rebel 编造 fabricate	
划	①huá	
	划不来 not worthwhile 划得来 worthwhile	
	划拳 play the finger-guessing game 划算 weigh	
	②huà	
	划分 divide 规划 plan	
刷	刷子 brush 牙刷 toothbrush 刷新 refresh	
制	制作 make 制冷 refrigeration 制定 formulate 制约 check	
	制止 stop 制订 draw up 复制 copy 特制 specially made	
	制品 products 法制 legal system 体制 system	
	编制 work out;establishment 专制 dictatorship	
	一国两制 one country, two systems	
创	创立 establish 创办 start and run（a business） 创建 found	
	创业 start an enterprise/business 创始 originate	
	创新 bring forth new ideas 首创 initiate	
节	细节 detail 情节 plot 礼节 rite 调节 regulate	
	节约 economize 节省 save 节能 save energy	
营	营救 rescue 野营 camping 经营 manage 国营 state-run	
	营业员 shop employees	
糟	一团糟 a terrible mess	
糕	糕点 refreshment 年糕 New Year cake 雪糕 ice cream	
抽	抽空 manage to find time 抽取 draw from 抽样 sample	
掉	掉头 turn round 掉色(shǎi) fade 擦掉 wipe off	
社	社会主义 socialism 社论 editorial 社会学 sociology	
	社会学家 sociologist 社交 social activities	
	出版社 publishing house 报社 press	
神	神经 nerve 神话 myth 神奇 magical 神气 spirited	
	神情 look 神态 expression 神色 expression 神圣 sacred	
却	忘却 forget 冷却 cool off 了却 fulfil	

既	既定　as decided　一如既往　always
册	一册书　a volume of book　注册　register　画册　album
	点名册　roll book
诞	诞生　be born　怪诞　queer　圣诞树　Christmas tree
圣	圣人　saint　圣母　the Virgin Mary　圣地　sacred place
横	横向　crosswise　横行　run wild
另	另一个　another　另一本　another book　另一件　another piece
	另一条　another article (of a document)　另一张　another piece of (paper)
拐	拐弯　turn a corner　拐角　corner　向左拐　turn left
引	引进　introduce　引用　quote from　引入　lead into　引号　lead
	引人入胜　fascinating　引人注目　eye-catching
乱	忙乱　busy and disorganized　乱七八糟　in great disorder
	手忙脚乱　in a flurry　以假乱真　mix the fake with the genuine
	出乱子　get into trouble　乱套　muddle things up

二　认读句子

Read and try to understand the following sentences.

1. 追求幸福是每个人的权利。
   It's the right of every person to pursue happiness.
2. 春节联欢晚会上表演的那个节目让很多人激动得掉下了眼泪。
   Many people were moved to tears by the program in the spring Festival Party.
3. 这个人不诚实,你可别受他的骗。
   That person is not honest and do not be taken in.
4. 这本旅游手册是旅行社发给大家的。
   This guidebook is handed out to each of you by the travel agency.
5. 我对中国文化很感兴趣。
   I am interested in Chinese culture.
6. 他最近创作了一篇小说,很受欢迎。
   He has recently finished writing a novel, which is very popular.
7. 你是不是对他有偏见? 我觉得你好像一直对他没有好感。
   Don't you think you're prejudiced against him? I feel that you seem to

have no good opinion of him all along.

8. 到了那个立交桥,再往右拐,你就可以看到建国门饭店。

When you reach the overpass and turn right, you will see the Jianguo Hotel.

9. 他喜欢紫色的东西,房间的地毯也是紫色的。

He likes things with the purple color, and even the carpet in his room is also purple.

10. 北京的名胜古迹很多。

Beijing boasts many historic relics.

11. 长城吸引了很多中外旅游者。

The Great Wall attracts a lot of foreign tourists as well as Chinese ones.

12. 你今天既然身体不好,就别跟我们去划船了。

Now that you are not well today, please do not come with us boating.

13. 他起床以后,连忙刷牙洗脸,连早饭也没吃就去学校了。

He hurried to wash his face and clean his teeth after he got up, and went to school without breakfast.

14. 那个工厂已经制造了一百万辆汽车。

The factory has already turned out one million automobiles.

15. 他在那次运动会上,创造了一百米游泳的最好成绩。

He created the best result in the one-hundred-meter swimming race in that game.

16. 本店营业时间从上午九点到下午六点。

This shop is open from 9 in the morning till 6 in the afternoon.

17. 在困难面前不能退却,应该想办法去克服。

We cannot beat a retreat in face of difficulty and should find ways to o-vercome them.

18. 我买了一本中国旅游手册,计划放假以后去南方旅游。

I've bought a guidebook about China and am planning to travel to the South.

19. 圣诞节是西方国家最重要的节日。

Christmas Day is the most important holiday in the West.

20. 他一连三次违反了公司制定的制度,所以老板让他下个月不用来上班了。

He has violated the system of the company three times in succession. So the boss told him that he needn't come to work next month.

21. 他住在郊区,上下班要花很多时间。

As he lives in the suburbs, it takes him a lot of time to travel between his work place and his home.

22. 这个红绿灯是不是坏了，我在<u>人行横道</u>边上等了十几分钟，红灯却一直没变。

I wonder if the traffic light works，because I have been waiting at the ze-bra crossing for over ten minutes but the red light has not changed yet.

23. 北京是<u>中华人民共和国</u>的首都。

Beijing is the capital of the People's Republic of China.

24. 他父母是<u>华侨</u>，所以他会说汉语。

His parents are overseas Chinese，and he can speak Chinese.

25. 请你用这个词另<u>造</u>一个句子。

Please make another sentence with this word.

26. 这是<u>圣经</u>里的一个故事。

This is a story from the Bible.

27. 这张桌子<u>横</u>过来放，放在靠近窗户的地方。

Turn the table crosswise and put it near the window.

28. 你先走吧，一会儿我<u>追</u>你。

Please go first，and I'll soon catch you up.

29. 你的桌子上怎么<u>乱七八糟</u>的？把这些东西摆放整齐！

How come your desk is in such a mess? Please put these things in order.

30. 真<u>糟糕</u>！我忘带钱包了。

What bad luck！I forgot to bring my wallet.

自学园地

Corner for Self-study

一　给下列词语注音

Mark the following words and thrases with phonetic symbols.

春节	计划	地毯	吸引	营业
(　)	(　)	(　)	(　)	(　)
热烈	社会	抽象	圣诞节	名胜古迹
(　)	(　)	(　)	(　)	(　)

二　写出本课含有下列偏旁的汉字并注音

Write out the characters with the following elements in this lesson, and mark them with phonetic symbols.

刂：_____（　　　）　_____（　　　）　_____（　　　）　_____（　　　）

辶：_____（　　　）　_____（　　　）　_____（　　　）　_____（　　　）

扌：_____（　　　）　_____（　　　）

亻：_____（　　　）　_____（　　　）

讠：_____（　　　）　_____（　　　）

礻：_____（　　　）　_____（　　　）

米：_____（　　　）　_____（　　　）

三　给下列汉字加上合适的部件，使它变成另一个汉字并注音

Add right components to the following characters to form new characters, and mark the new ones with phonetic symbols.

舌 ⟶ _____（　　　）　　弓 ⟶ _____（　　　）　　册 ⟶ _____（　　　）

黄 ⟶ _____（　　　）　　既 ⟶ _____（　　　）　　另 ⟶ _____（　　　）

却 ⟶ _____（　　　）　　土 ⟶ _____（　　　）　　告 ⟶ _____（　　　）

此 ⟶ _____（　　　）　　因 ⟶ _____（　　　）　　交 ⟶ _____（　　　）

四　在括号内加上合适的词语

Fill in the blanks with right words and phrases.

（　　　　）的圣诞节　　　（　　　　）的精神　　　（　　　　）的计划

（　　　　）的兴趣　　　（　　　　）的节目　　　（　　　　）的社会

诚实的（　　　）　　　乱糟糟的（　　　）　　　抽象的（　　　）

紫色的（　　　）　　　营业的（　　　）　　　创作的（　　　）

五 阅读下列句子并回答问题

Read the following sentences and answer the questions accordingly.

1. 你这么给孩子们<u>解释</u>太<u>抽象</u>了,他们怎么可能听得懂呢?
   孩子们听得懂他的解释吗? 为什么?

2. 真没想到,经过一年多的<u>改造</u>,以前那个<u>乱糟糟</u>的市场现在<u>却</u>变成了一家
   大超市,里边的商品<u>既</u>丰富又便宜。
   这儿以前是什么地方?

3. 医生告诉他:"你要再<u>抽</u>这么多烟,就只有死路一条。"
   他还能不能抽这么多烟?

4. <u>兴趣</u>是最好的老师,因为这些活动<u>引</u>起了孩子们的<u>兴趣</u>,他们才会愿意去
   研究,去<u>创造</u>,而这种创造精神是非常宝贵的。
   孩子们的创造精神与兴趣有什么关系?

5. 你的衣服怎么穿得这么脏,这些脏的地方怎么洗都<u>洗不掉</u>。
   洗过以后,衣服还脏吗?

6. 他刚大学毕业,<u>社会</u>经验不足,所以容易<u>受骗</u>。
   他为什么容易受骗?

7. 迈克尔·<u>乔丹</u>的到来,<u>吸引</u>了大批的球迷,那些<u>追星族</u>们,为了见他一面,
   已经在那个篮球场外<u>连续</u>等候好几个小时了,当时的场面有点<u>乱</u>。
   球迷在篮球场外做什么?

8. 今天别<u>AA</u>制了,今天我请客,小姐,你们这儿可以<u>刷卡</u>吗?
   他们现在可能在哪儿?

9. <u>春节</u>、国庆节、五一节、中秋节都是中国重要的节日,除<u>中秋节</u>外,节日期
   间会放假,<u>中秋节</u>的时候,工作的单位或生活的<u>社区</u>,一般会发一些<u>中秋</u>
   节吃的月饼。
   中秋节放假吗? 中秋节吃什么?

10. 秋天是北京最好的<u>季节</u>,不冷也不热,在这个<u>季节</u>,常常会<u>吸引</u>大批的旅
    游者前来游览北京的<u>名胜古迹</u>。
    什么时候游览北京最好? 为什么?

第九课

汉字园地
Corner for Chinese Characters

1.	亭	tíng	pavilion
	亭子	tíngzi	pavilion
2.	停	tíng	stop; pause
	不停	bù tíng	continue
	停止	tíngzhǐ	stop
3.	洲	zhōu	continent
	亚洲	Yàzhōu	Asia
4.	史	shǐ	history
	历史	lìshǐ	history
5.	驶	shǐ	(of vehicles) go
	驾驶	jiàshǐ	drive; steer; pilot
	驾驶员	jiàshǐyuán	driver
6.	普	pǔ	common
	普通	pǔtōng	common
	普遍	pǔbiàn	universal
7.	谱	pǔ	score
	菜谱	càipǔ	menu
8.	竟	jìng	unexpectedly
	究竟	jiūjìng	exactly
	竟然	jìngrán	go so far as to

9. 境	jìng	situation
国境	guójìng	national border
10. 镜	jìng	mirror
眼镜	yǎnjìng	spectacles
墨镜	mòjìng	sunglasses
11. 景	jǐng	scene
风景	fēngjǐng	landscape
情景	qíngjǐng	scene;situation
12. 惊	jīng	alarm
吃惊	chī jīng	be alarmed
13. 转	①zhuǎn	turn
转变	zhuǎnbiàn	change;transform
转告	zhuǎngào	relay a message to
	②zhuàn	turn
转动	zhuàndòng	turn;rotate
14. 传	①chuán	pass on
传播	chuánbō	spread
传说	chuánshuō	legend
	②zhuàn	biography
自传	zìzhuàn	autobiography
15. 担	dān	carry
担心	dānxīn	be worried
担任	dānrèn	hold the post of
16. 胆	dǎn	gallbladder
大胆	dàdǎn	bold
胆小	dǎn xiǎo	timid
17. 召	zhào	call
召开	zhàokāi	open(a meeting，etc.)

号召	hàozhào	call on
18. 招	zhāo	wave;beckon
打招呼	dǎ zhāohu	greet
招待	zhāodài	receive (guests)
招待会	zhāodàihuì	reception
19. 脾	pí	spleen
脾气	píqi	temperament
20. 环	huán	cirde
环境	huánjìng	environment
21. 怀	huái	bosom;keep in mind
怀念	huáiniàn	cherish the memory of
22. 倍	bèi	-fold
加倍	jiābèi	double
23. 陪	péi	accompany
陪同	péitóng	companion
24. 赔	péi	compensate
赔钱	péi qián	lose money
25. 培	péi	bring up
培养	péiyǎng	cultivate
26. 缺	quē	lack
缺少	quēshǎo	lack
缺点	quēdiǎn	shortcoming
27. 嫂	sǎo	sister-in-law
嫂子	sǎozi	sister-in-law
28. 何	hé	what
任何	rènhé	any
如何	rúhé	how;what
29. 副	fù	set;pair;deputy

	一副眼镜	yí fù yǎnjìng	a pair of glasses
	副食	fùshí	non-staple food
30.	亚	yà	second; inferior
	亚军	yàjūn	runner-up
31.	凡	fán	any
	凡是	fánshì	any
32.	之	zhī	a function word, it
	之间	zhī jiān	between
	之前	zhīqián	before
	之后	zhīhòu	after
	之上	zhī shàng	above
	之下	zhī xià	under
	之内	zhī nèi	within
	之外	zhī wài	beyond
	之中	zhī zhōng	in
	之一	zhī yī	one of
	百分之……	bǎi fēn zhī…	percent
	总之	zǒngzhī	in a word
33.	乏	fá	lack
	缺乏	quēfá	lack
34.	于	yú	at; in
	关于	guānyú	about
	对于	duìyú	with regard to
	等于	děngyú	equal
	于是	yúshì	hence
35.	由	yóu	from; by
	由于	yóuyú	since; as; because
	自由	zìyóu	freedom; free
36.	丈	zhàng	senior; $3\frac{1}{3}$ metres
	丈夫	zhàngfu	husband

记忆窍门

Tips for Memorizing Work

一 **形声字声旁记忆**

Memorize the following characters with the given phonetic elements.

亭　tíng

（ˊ）	亭	pavilion	亭子	tíngzi	pavilion
（ˊ）	停	stop；pause	不停	bù tíng	continue
			停止	tíngzhǐ	stop

州　zhōu

| （　） | 州 | | | | |
| （ˉ） | 洲 | continent | 亚洲 | Yàzhōu | Asia |

史　shǐ

（ˇ）	史	history	历史	lìshǐ	history
（ˇ）	驶	go	驾驶	jiàshǐ	drive
			驾驶员	jiàshǐyuán	driver
（　）	使				

普　pǔ

（ˇ）	普	common	普通	pǔtōng	common
			普遍	pǔbiàn	universal
（ˇ）	谱	score	菜谱	càipǔ	menu

竟　jìng

（ˋ）	竟	unexpectedly	究竟	jiūjìng	exactly
			竟然	jìngrán	go so far as to
（ˋ）	境	situation	国境	guójìng	national border
（ˋ）	镜	mirror	眼镜	yǎnjìng	spectacles
			墨镜	mòjìng	sunglasses

京	jīng				
	（ˇ）	景	scene	风景 fēngjǐng	landscape
	（ˉ）	惊	alarm	吃惊 chījīng	be alarmed
				情景 qíngjǐng	scene；situation
	（ ）	影	_____		

专	zhuān				
	（ˉ）	专	_____		
	（ˇ）	转	turn	转变 zhuǎnbiàn	change
				转告 zhuǎngào	relay a message to
	（ˋ）	转	turn	转动 zhuàndòng	rotate
	（ˋ）	传	biography	自传 zìzhuàn	autobiography
	(chuán)	传	pass on	传播 chuánbō	spread
				传说 chuánshuō	legend

旦	dàn				
	（ ）	旦	_____		
	（ ）	但	_____		
	（ˉ）	担	carry	担心 dānxīn	be worried
				担任 dānrèn	hold the post of
	（ˇ）	胆	gallbladder	大胆 dàdǎn	bold
				胆小 dǎnxiǎo	timid

召	zhào				
	（ ）	照	_____		
	（ ）	绍	_____		
	（ˋ）	召		召开 zhàokāi	open
				号召 hàozhào	call on
	（ˉ）	招	wave；beckon	打招呼 dǎ zhāohu	greet
				招待 zhāodài	receive (guests)
				招待会 zhāodàihuì	reception

亭 停 洲 史 驶 普 谱 竟 境 镜 景 惊 转 传

担 胆 召 招

二　比较同音、近音字

Compare the following characters with same or similar pronunciation.

啤——脾

啤					
脾	pí	spleen	脾气	píqi	temperament

还——坏——环——怀

还					
坏					
环	huán	circle	环境	huánjìng	environment
怀	huái	bosom；keep in mind			
			怀念	huáiniàn	cherish a memory of

倍——陪——赔——培

倍	bèi	-fold	加倍	jiābèi	double
陪	péi	accompany	陪同	péitóng	accompany
赔	péi	compensate	赔钱	péi qián	lose money
培	péi	bring up	培养	péiyǎng	cultivate

决——缺

决					
缺	quē	lack	缺少	quēshǎo	lack
			缺点	quēdiǎn	short coming

瘦——嫂

瘦					
嫂	sǎo	sister-in-law	嫂子	sǎozi	sister-in-law

河——何

河					
何	hé	what	任何	rènhé	any
			如何	rúhé	how；what

富——福——副

富					

福 _____

副　fù　　set；pair；deputy　一副眼镜　yí fù yǎnjìng　a pair of glasses
　　　　　　　　　　　　　副食　fùshí　　　non-staple food

脾	环	怀	倍	陪	赔	培	缺	嫂	何	副

三　比较下列形近字

Compare the following characters with similar pictographic elements.

业——亚

业 _____
亚　yà　　second；inferior　亚军　yàjūn　　　　runner-up

几——凡

几 _____
凡　fán　any　　　　　　　凡是　fánshì　　　any

之——乏

之　zhī　a function word，it　之间　zhī jiān　　between
　　　　　　　　　　　　　　　之前　zhīqián　　before
　　　　　　　　　　　　　　　之后　zhīhòu　　after
　　　　　　　　　　　　　　　之上　zhī shàng　above
　　　　　　　　　　　　　　　之下　zhī xià　　under
　　　　　　　　　　　　　　　之内　zhī nèi　　within
　　　　　　　　　　　　　　　之外　zhī wài　　beyond
　　　　　　　　　　　　　　　之中　zhī zhōng　in
　　　　　　　　　　　　　　　之一　zhī yī　　　one of
　　　　　　　　　　　　　　　百分之……　bǎi fēn zhī…　percent
　　　　　　　　　　　　　　　总之　zǒngzhī　　in a word
乏　fá　lack　　　　　　　缺乏　quēfá　　　lack

干——于

干 _____
于　yú　　at；in　　　　　关于　guānyú　　about
　　　　　　　　　　　　　对于　duìyú　　　with regard to

等于	děngyú	equal
于是	yúshì	hence

田——由

田 _____

由	yóu	from; by	由于	yóuyú	since
			自由	zìyóu	freedom

大——丈

大 _____

| 丈 | zhàng | senior; $3\frac{1}{3}$ metres | 丈夫 | zhàngfu | husband |

亚	凡	之	乏	于	由	丈

活用园地

Corner for Flexible Usage

一 组词

Form words and phrases.

亭	食品亭 food kiosk 书报亭 book kiosk 凉亭 kiosk
停	停留 stay 停工 stop work 停电 cut off electricity supply
	停水 cut off water supply 停车 stop a car
	停职 suspend one from one's duty 停业 close down
洲	非洲 Africa 北美洲 North America 南美洲 South America
	大洋州 Oceania 南极洲 Antarctica 欧洲 Europe
史	史学 historiography 史料 historical data
	史书 historical records
驶	行驶 go
普	普及 popularize 普查 general survey
	科普 pop science 吉普车 jeep 普通话 common speech

谱　乐谱　music score　食谱　menu　棋谱　chess manual
　　年谱　chronological life　家谱　genealogy

竟　竟敢　actually dare　毕竟　after all　究竟　actually

境　入境　enter a country　边境　border area
　　离境　depart from a country　处境　situation
　　心境　state of mind　境界　state　境内　within boundaries of
　　困境　difficult position

镜　镜子　mirror　镜片　lens　镜头　scene　望远镜　telescope
　　放大镜　magnifier　哈哈镜　distorting mirror

景　景色　view　景象　scene　景物　scenery　背景　background
　　全景　overall view　场景　scene　美景　beautiful scenery
　　前景　prospect　夜景　night view

惊　受惊　be alarmed　惊奇　wonder　惊喜　delightful surprise
　　惊动　startle　惊人　surprising　惊险　excitingly dangerous

专　专心　be bent on　专一　set one's mind on　专门　special
　　专业　speciality　专利　patent　专长　speciality
　　专科　specialized subject

转　①zhuǎn
　　转播　relay　转入　shift to　转换　exchange
　　转交　hand over　转化　transform　转身　turn one's body
　　转让　transfer　转弯　turn　转达　pass on
　　好转　turn for the better　转向　change direction
　　②zhuàn
　　转椅　swivel　转向　lose direction　转来转去　turn about

传　chuán
　　传呼　pass on a telephone message or call someone to answer the
　　phone　传真　fax　传播　disseminate　流传　spread　传达　convey
　　传递　transmit　传染　infect　传递　carry　传单　leaflet

担　担任　be appointed as　担负　shoulder　负担　burden

胆　胆子　guts　胆大　bold　胆量　courage　胆敢　dare　大胆　bold

但　但愿　wish　不但　not only

召　召集　call together　感召　move and inspire

招　招收　recruit　招生　enroll new students
　　招聘　invite applications for a job　招手　wave

脾 牛脾气 stubbornness　坏脾气 bad temper　发脾气 lose one's temper

环 环节 link　环球 round the globe　环视 look around
耳环 ear ring　花环 wreath　光环 light ring
环行 going in a ring　四周环山 surrounded by mountains on all sides

怀 关怀 concern

倍 一倍 onefold　两倍 twofold　十倍 tenfold
事半功倍 get twice the result with half the effort
事倍功半 get half the result with twice the effort

陪 失陪 excuse me

赔 赔本 lose money　赔礼 apologize　退赔 return
赔不是 make an apology

培 培育 cultivate

缺 缺课 absent from classes　缺人 be short of hands　缺口 gap
短缺 shortage　完美无缺 perfect

嫂 空嫂 air lady　月嫂 confinement caring woman

何 无论无何 in any case　何人 who　何时 what time
何处 where　何必 why　何况 let alone　何等 how
为何 why

副 两副手套 two pairs of gloves　一副笑脸 a smiling face
副主任 deputy director　副业 side occupation
副作用 by-effect　副词 adverb

亚 东亚 East Asia　西亚 West Asia　南亚 South Asia
亚热带 semitropics

凡 非凡 extraordinary　凡人 ordinary person　平凡 ordinary
凡事 everything　凡士林 Vaseline

之 百分之五 five percent　十分之九 nine tenths
反之 on the contrary　无价之宝 treasure of treasures

乏 乏味 boring　解乏 get rid of fatigue

于 大于 bigger than　小于 smaller than　生于 be born in
便于 convenient for　急于 anxious to do　过于 over
在于 in　至于 as for　位于 be located　处于 in a state of...
敢于 dare to

由 由此可见 thus it can be seen

丈 老丈人 father-in-law　丈母娘 mother-in-law

二 认读句子

Read and try to understand the following sentences.

1. 中国位于亚洲东部。

China is situated in East Asia.

2. 关于中国的历史，我了解得不多。

I do not know much about China's history.

3. 他是一个老驾驶员了，经验很丰富。

He's a veteran driver with rich experience.

4. 在中国，很多地方的人也说不好普通话。

In China people from many places cannot speak *putonghua* properly either.

5. 先生，这是菜谱，你先看看要什么菜。

Here's the menu, sir. Please have a look and give your order.

6. 那个戴一副墨镜的人是她的丈夫。

The man with a pair of sunglasses is her husband.

7. 由于他胆子小，所以很少说话。

As he is timid, he is rather tacit.

8. 我不知道怎么办入境手续。

I have no idea as how to go through the formalities for entry.

9. 不知为何，这些天她常发脾气。

She's been bad tempered these days, and nobody knows why.

10. 这个城市风景很美，环境不错。

The city is beautiful with good natural environment.

11. 让人吃惊，她们竟然取得了世界亚军。

To the surprise of everyone, they should have won the second place in the world competition.

12. 阿里不在，他刚出去，有什么事需要我转告吗？

Ali is not in. He went out just now. Is there any message for him?

13. 别担心，你的病休息几天就会好的。

Don't worry. You'll be well again after a few days' rest.

14. 地球一直在不停地运转着。

The earth keeps revolving.

15. 他决定，退休之后写一本自传。

He has decided to write an autobiography after retirement.

16. 明天下午两点,学校召开一个汉语学习讨论会。

The school is holding a symposium on Chinese learning at 2 p. m. tomorrow.

17. 中国人常常怎么跟人打招呼?

How do the Chinese people greet one another?

18. 我很怀念我的亲人和朋友。

I miss my folks and friends.

19. 按规定,任何人卖假货,都要加倍赔钱。

According to the regulations, you'll have to double your compensation for the fake goods you sell.

20. 那位专家陪同外国客人去上海了。

The specialist accompanied foreign guests to Shanghai.

21. 她父母都是音乐教师,所以从小就培养了她对音乐的兴趣。

Both her parents are music teachers, and that is why they cultivated her interest in music from childhood.

22. 这个房间里还缺少一台冰箱。

This room needs a fridge.

23. 他嫂子结婚之前是一个护士。

His sister-in-law was a nurse before her marriage.

24. 我弟弟喜欢音乐,但是我对音乐却缺乏兴趣。

My younger brother loves music, but I lack enthusiasm for it.

25. 凡是喜欢足球的人,都知道贝利。

Anyone who loves football knows about Berry.

26. 在中国,有很多关于月亮的传说。

There are a lot of legends about the moon in China.

27. 中国人口几乎是世界人口的四分之一。

China's population almost makes up one fourth of the world's total.

28. 有的人喜欢运动,有的人喜欢旅游,总之,各人有各人的爱好。

Some love sports, and some love travel. In a word, every one has his own hobby.

29. 好久不见,近况如何?

Haven't seen you for ages. How are things with you?

30. 他成绩不好,因为他对学习缺乏决心和信心。

He got bad results in his studies for he lacked determination and confidence.

自学园地
Corner for Self-study

一　给下列词语注音

Mark the following words with phonetic symbols.

停止　　　　普通　　　　吃惊　　　　缺乏　　　　传说
（　　　）　（　　　）　（　　　）　（　　　）　（　　　）

加倍　　　　墨镜　　　　传播　　　　赔钱　　　　担心
（　　　）　（　　　）　（　　　）　（　　　）　（　　　）

二　根据意思把左右两栏用线连起来

Link the word in the left column with the one in the right column that matches it in meaning.

驾驶　　　　态度　　　　　　　　普遍的　　　　风景
转变　　　　客人　　　　　　　　美丽的　　　　传说
召开　　　　汽车　　　　　　　　安静的　　　　脾气
招待　　　　学生　　　　　　　　古老的　　　　情况
培养　　　　信心　　　　　　　　古怪的　　　　环境
缺乏　　　　会议

三　选择下列句子中"于"的含义（在句子后面的括号内填上各义项的序号）

Fill in the blanks with the numbers of the meanings of"于"in the following sentences.

①在　　　②对　　　③向　　　④从　　　⑤比　　　⑥给

1. 新中国于 1949 年 10 月 1 日成立，今年是国庆五十六周年。　　　（　　　）
2. 史先生去年毕业于北京大学中文系，是博士生。　　　（　　　）
3. 吸烟不利于健康。　　　（　　　）
4. 你的来信已于昨日收到。　　　（　　　）

5. 系主任今年要退休了,他说:"早点儿让位<u>于</u>年轻人,他们会比我干得更好。" （　　）

6. 孩子今年的成绩好<u>于</u>去年。 （　　）

7. 遇到生词的时候,我常求(qiú,ask)助<u>于</u>词典,所以这本词典是我最好的老师。 （　　）

四　选择填空

Choose the right characters to fill in the blanks.

1. 他嫂子的_____气特别好,从来不跟人生气。 （啤、牌、脾）

2. 最近几年,出_____旅行的人数在不断上升。 （镜、境、竟）

3. 刚才我在路上看到你,还跟你打了一声_____呼,可是你没听见。 （照、召、招、绍）

4. 我们会加_____努力,争取_____养出更多更好的学生。 （培、陪、赔、倍）

5. 你的_____子也太小了,这种游戏(game)都不敢玩。 （但、担、胆）

6. 这个地方_____水,自然环_____比较差。 （决、缺、块）（境、镜）

五　阅读下列句子并回答问题

Read the following sentences and answer the questions accordingly.

1. 现在谁也搞不清楚,这件事<u>对于</u>我们来说,<u>究竟</u>是好事还是坏事。
"我们"搞不清楚什么?

2. 看到这种<u>情况</u>,我很吃惊,一夜<u>之间</u>,他的态度<u>竟然</u>发生了180度的<u>转变</u>。
他的态度有没有变化?

3. 调查发现,在这个中学的初中部,有<u>百分之五十四</u>的学生戴上了近视<u>眼镜</u>。
<u>这</u>些学生眼睛怎么了?

4. 怕吃苦,这是现在这些孩子<u>普遍</u>的<u>缺点</u>,这就是<u>为何</u>有那么多的父母想让他们的孩子参加今年夏天的"吃苦夏令营"的原因之一。
父母为何让孩子参加"吃苦夏令营"?

5. 这次考试规定在两个小时<u>之内</u>完成,请大家抓紧时间。
这次考试有多长时间?

6. <u>关于</u>这个问题,外交部今天上午<u>召</u>开了一个记者<u>招</u>待会,一会儿电视里有<u>转</u>播。

我想了解记者招待会的情况,应该怎么办?

7. 自从他<u>担</u>任市长职务以来,积极<u>号召</u>全市人民参加绿化城市的活动,经过几年的努力,城市的<u>环境</u>有了很大的<u>改变</u>。

城市环境为何有了很大的改变?

8. 未经同意,<u>任何</u>人不得入内。

什么人可以进去?

第十课

汉字园地
Corner for Chinese Characters

1.	吓	xià	frighten
	吓死	xiàsǐ	be frightened to death
2.	笨	bèn	stupid
	笨手笨脚	bèn shǒu bèn jiǎo	clumsy
	笨蛋	bèndàn	idiot
3.	效	xiào	effect
	效果	xiàoguǒ	effect
	有效	yǒuxiào	effective; valid
4.	列	liè	line
	列车	lièchē	train
	系列	xìliè	set; series
	下列	xiàliè	the following
5.	烈	liè	scorching
	热烈	rèliè	warm
	激烈	jīliè	fierce
6.	例	lì	example
	举例(子)	jǔ lì(zi)	take something as an example
	例如	lìrú	for example
	比例	bǐlì	proportion

7.	焦	jiāo	scorched
	焦急	jiāojí	worried
8.	瞧	qiáo	look
	小瞧	xiǎoqiáo	look down upon
9.	龄	líng	age；years
	年龄	niánlíng	age
10.	领	lǐng	collar；lead
	本领	běnlǐng	ability
	领带	lǐngdài	tie
	白领	báilǐng	white-collar
11.	邻	lín	neighbour
	邻居	línjū	neighbour
12.	睁	zhēng	open wide
	睁开	zhēngkāi	open
13.	筝	zhēng	kite
	风筝	fēngzheng	kite
14.	挣	zhèng	struggle to get free；earn
	挣钱	zhèng qián	make money
15.	导	dǎo	guide
	领导	lǐngdǎo	lead；leader
	报导	bàodǎo	report；news report
	导游	dǎoyóu	tourist guide
16.	异	yì	different
	异常	yìcháng	unusual
17.	扔	rēng	throw
	扔垃圾	rēng lājī	throw away garbage
18.	仍	réng	yet
	仍然	réngrán	still

19. 喊	hǎn	shout
叫喊	jiàohǎn	yell
20. 憾	hàn	regret
遗憾	yíhàn	regret
21. 减	jiǎn	decrease
减少	jiǎnshǎo	cut down
减轻	jiǎnqīng	lighten
减肥	jiǎnféi	lose weight
27. 线	xiàn	thread
路线	lùxiàn	route
光线	guāngxiàn	ray
热线	rèxiàn	hot line; busy route
23. 践	jiàn	trample
实践	shíjiàn	practice
24. 贱	jiàn	cheap
贱卖	jiàn mài	be sold cheap
25. 燥	zào	dry
干燥	gānzào	dry
26. 噪	zào	noisy
噪音	zàoyīn	noise
27. 躁	zào	rash; restless
急躁	jízào	impatient
28. 遗	yí	lose; bequeath
遗产	yíchǎn	legacy
29. 显	xiǎn	show; obvious
显得	xiǎnde	look
显然	xiǎnrán	obviously
30. 终	zhōng	end
终于	zhōngyú	in the end
始终	shǐzhōng	from beginning to end

31.	充	chōng	fill
	充满	chōngmǎn	be full of
	充足	chōngzú	ample
	充分	chōngfèn	sufficient
32.	统	tǒng	rule
	总统	zǒngtǒng	president
	统一	tǒngyī	unify; unified
	系统	xìtǒng	system
33.	省	shěng	province; save
	节省	jiéshěng	economize
34.	曾	céng	once
	曾经	céngjīng	once
35.	增	zēng	add
	增加	zēngjiā	increase
36.	亩	mǔ	*mu*
	英亩	yīngmǔ	acre
37.	际	jì	inter-
	实际	shíjì	reality; real
	国际	guójì	international
	交际	jiāojì	contact; communication
38.	标	biāo	mark
	标准	biāozhǔn	standard
	标点	biāodiǎn	punctuation
	目标	mùbiāo	target
	标语	biāoyǔ	slogan
	标志	biāozhì	mark; sign

记忆窍门

Tips for Memorizing Work

一 形声字声旁记忆

Memorize the following characters with the given phonetic elements.

下　xià

（丶）吓　frighten　　　吓死　xiàsǐ　　　　be frightened to death

本　běn

（丶）笨　stupid　　　笨手笨脚　bèn shǒu bèn jiǎo　　clumsy
　　　　　　　　　　　笨蛋　bèndàn　　　　　idiot

交　jiāo

（　）校　＿＿＿＿＿＿＿＿＿＿＿＿＿＿＿＿

（xiào）效　effect　　　效果　xiàoguǒ　　effect
　　　　　　　　　　　有效　yǒuxiào　　effective；valid

（　）咬　＿＿＿＿＿＿＿＿＿＿＿＿＿＿＿＿

列　liè

（丶）列　line　　　列车　lièchē　　　train
　　　　　　　　　系列　xìliè　　　set；series
　　　　　　　　　下列　xiàliè　　　the following

（丶）烈　scorching　　热烈　rèliè　　warm
　　　　　　　　　　激烈　jīliè　　fierce

（lì）例　example　　举例（子）　jǔ lì(zi)
　　　　　　　　　例如　lìrú　　　for example
　　　　　　　　　比例　bǐlì　　　proportion

焦　jiāo

（　）蕉　＿＿＿＿＿＿＿＿＿＿＿＿＿＿＿＿

（‾）焦　scorched　　焦急　jiāojí　　worried

| （qiáo）瞧 | look | 小瞧 | xiǎoqiáo | look down upon |

令　lìng

（ ）	零	_____			
（ˊ）	龄	age；years	年龄	niánlíng	age
（ˇ）	领	collar；lead	本领	běnlǐng	ability
			领带	lǐngdài	tie
			白领	báilǐng	white-collar
（lín）	邻	neighbour	邻居	línjū	neighbour

争　zhēng

（ ）	争	_____			
（ˉ）	睁	open wide	睁开	zhēngkāi	open one's eyes
（ˉ）	筝	kite	风筝	fēngzheng	kite
（ˋ）	挣	struggle to get free；earn			
			挣钱	zhèng qián	earn money

| 吓 | 笨 | 效 | 列 | 烈 | 例 | 焦 | 瞧 | 龄 | 领 | 邻 | 睁 | 筝 | 挣 |

二　比较下列形近字

Compare the following characters with similar pictographic elements.

导——异

导	dǎo	guide	领导	lǐngdǎo	lead；leader
			报导	bàodǎo	report；news report
			导游	dǎoyóu	tourist guide
异	yì	different	异常	yìcháng	unusual

扔——仍

| 扔 | rēng | throw | 扔垃圾 | rēng lājī | throw away garbage |
| 仍 | réng | yet | 仍然 | réngrán | still |

喊——憾——减

| 喊 | hǎn | shout | 叫喊 | jiàohǎn | shout |
| 憾 | hàn | regret | 遗憾 | yíhàn | regret |

减	jiǎn	decrease	减少	jiǎnshǎo	cut down
			减轻	jiǎnqīng	lighten
			减肥	jiǎnféi	lose weight

钱——浅——线

钱	_____
浅	_____
线	xiàn	thread	路线	lùxiàn	route
			光线	guāngxiàn	ray of light
			热线	rèxiàn	hot line; busy route

践——贱

践	jiàn	trample	实践	shíjiàn	practice
贱	jiàn	cheap	贱卖	jiàn mài	be sold cheap

操——澡——燥——噪——躁

操	_____
澡	_____
燥	zào	dry	干燥	gānzào	dry
噪	zào	noisy	噪音	zàoyīn	noise
躁	zào	rash; restless	急躁	jízào	impatient

导	异	扔	仍	喊	憾	减	线	践	贱	燥	噪	躁

三　基本字带字

Memorize the following characters with the given basic elements.

贵——遗

贵	_____
遗	yí		遗产	yíchǎn	legacy

业——显

业	_____
显	xiǎn		显得	xiǎnde	look
			显然	xiǎnrán	obviously

冬——终

| 终 | zhōng | 终于 | zhōngyú | in the end |
| | | 始终 | shǐzhōng | from beginning to end |

充——统

充	chōng	充满	chōngmǎn	be full of
		充足	chōngzú	ample
		充分	chōngfèn	sufficient
统	tǒng	总统	zǒngtǒng	president
		统一	tǒngyī	unify；unified
		系统	xìtǒng	system

少——省

| 省 | shěng | 节省 | jiéshěng | save |

曾——增

| 曾 | céng | 曾经 | céngjīng | once |
| 增 | zēng | 增加 | zēngjiā | increase |

田——亩

| 亩 | mǔ | 英亩 | yīngmǔ | acre |

示——际——标

际	jì	实际	shíjì	reality；real
		国际	guójì	international
		交际	jiāojì	contact；communication
标	biāo	标准	biāozhǔn	standard
		标点	biāodiǎn	punctuation
		目标	mùbiāo	target
		标语	biāoyǔ	slogan
		标志	biāozhì	mark；sign

遗 显 终 充 统 省 曾 增 亩 际 标

活用园地

Corner for Flexible Usage

 组词

Form words and phrases.

吓	惊吓 frighten	吓倒 frighten
笨	笨重 cumbersome	笨鸟先飞 the slow need to start early
效	效力 effect 见效 become effective 无效 invalid	
	生效 take effect 失效 be no longer effective 特效 special effect	
列	并列 parallel 行列 line 排列 arrange 前列 forefront	
	系列 series 列举 make a list of 一列火车 a train	
烈	烈酒 strong alcoholic 烈火 scorching fire	
	烈日 scorching sun 烈士 martyr 兴高采烈 extremely happy	
例	例句 illustrative sentence 例题 illustrative problem	
	例子 example 例外 exception 惯例 usual practice	
	条例 rules 下不为例 not to be repeated 史无前例 unprecedented	
焦	焦点 focus	
瞧	瞧见 see 瞧得起 have a good opinion of	
	瞧不起 look down upon	
龄	教龄 years of teaching 学龄 school age	
	军龄 years with the army 艺龄 years of stage career	
	婚龄 marriage age 高龄 venerable age	
领	领先 be in the lead 领土 territory 领会 understand	
	带领 lead 首领 leader 蓝领 blue-collar 黑领 black-collar	
	粉(fěn)领 pink-collar 金领 gold-collar	
邻	邻国 neighboring country 邻村 neighboring village	
	邻近 be near to	
导	导师 teacher 导演 direct; director 教导 instruct	
	向导 guide 引导 guide 辅导 coach	
异	惊异(jīngyì) amazed 差异 difference	

	异口同声	with one voice	日新月异	change daily					
	大同小异	basically the same with insignificant difference							
扔	扔掉	throw away	扔石头	throw stones	扔果皮	littering			
	扔球	throw a ball							
仍	仍旧	still							
喊	呼喊	shout	大喊	cry aloud	哭喊	cry	喊叫	yell	叫喊 shout
憾	缺憾	regret	遗憾	regret					
减	减产	drop in production	减轻	alleviate	减低	lower			
	减法	subtraction	减价	lower the prices	减员	depletion of numbers			
	减少	decrease							
线	线条	line	有线电视	cable TV	航线	navigation course			
	毛线	wool	直线	straight line	电线	electric wire			
	曲线	curve	地平线	horizon	紫外线	ultraviolet ray			
贱	下贱	cheap	低贱	low and cheap	贵贱	noble or humble			
澡	擦澡	rub oneself down with a wet towel	澡堂	public baths					
燥	燥热	hot and dry	干燥	dry					
噪	噪声	noise							
躁	毛躁	rash	烦躁	agitated					
遗	遗留	leave over	遗传	inherit	遗失	lose	遗体	remains	
	遗址	site	遗书	posthumous writings					
	遗言	words at one's death bed							
显	显示	demonstrate	显得	appear	浅显	easy and simple			
	显而易见	obvious							
终	终点	finish	终身	all one's life	终止	end	终究	after all	
	终年	throughout the year	终生	all one's life	最终	eventually			
	有始有终	finish anything once something is started							
	自始至终	from beginning to end							
充	充分	fully	充实	full	充足	ample	充当	serve as	
	冒充	pretend to be							
统	统计	statistics	统治	rule	统一	unify	传统	tradition	
	系统	system							
省	省力	save labor	省钱	save money	省时	save time			
	省得	in order not to	省会	provincial capital					
	省长	governor of a province							

增	增进 promote　增产 increase production　增光 add honor to
	增减 increase and decrease　增长 growth
际	校际 interschool　人际 interpersonal
	一望无际 stretch as far as the eye can reach
标	标题 title　音标 phonetic symbol　商标 trademark
	路标 road sign　光标 cursor　标准间 standard room

二　认读句子

Read and try to understand the following sentences.

1. 他在我背后<u>大喊</u>一声,<u>吓死</u>我了。
   He gave out a sudden cry behind me, which almost scared me to death.

2. 这种药我<u>曾经</u>吃过,<u>效果</u>不错。
   I've taken such medicine, and it's effective.

3. 我还不懂这两个词之间的<u>差异</u>,你能不能再举一个<u>例子</u>?
   I don't understand the difference between the two words. Can you give me another example?

4. 比赛快开始了,他们还没来,我心里<u>焦急</u>死了。
   The match is going to start soon and yet they are not here. I'm really worried.

5. <u>列车</u>开过来了。
   The train is coming.

6. 他的病<u>终于</u>好了。
   At last he got well again.

7. 他早把这件事<u>扔</u>到脑后了。
   He's completely forgotten about it.

8. 你可别<u>小瞧</u>他,他虽然<u>年龄</u>小,本领却不小,参加了很多次<u>国际</u>比赛。
   Don't look down upon him. Young as he is, he has taken part in many of the international competitions.

9. 这些<u>领带</u>已经<u>贱卖</u>了,才二十五元钱一条,却<u>仍然</u>没人来买。
   These ties are already sold cheap, only ￥25 a piece, but still nobody is interested.

10. 早上八点,我睡醒了,<u>睁开</u>眼睛一看,房间<u>里充满</u>阳光,又是一个好天气。
    I woke up at 8 in the morning. I opened my eyes to find the room full of sunshine. It was another fine day.

11. 有很多孩子在那儿放<u>风筝</u>，他们<u>显得异常</u>地高兴。

Many children are flying kites there, and they look extremely happy.

12. <u>毕业</u>以后，我要努力工作，努力<u>挣钱</u>。

After graduation, I'll work hard to earn money.

13. 这包菜已经坏了，<u>扔掉</u>吧。

The bag of vegetable has gone bad. Let's throw it away.

14. 真<u>遗憾</u>，他不能来参加我们的晚会了。

It is a pity that the he cannot join us at the party.

15. 最近我父母<u>减少</u>了我的生活费，所以我花钱的时候要节省一点儿。

Recently, my parents have cut down my living expenses, and I have to be economical.

16. 这个房间的<u>光线</u>太黑，外面的噪音也很大，你能不能给我换一个房间？

It's too dark inside the room, and it's very noisy outside. Can you give me another room?

17. 他<u>显然</u>是在骗你。你别忘了，他这个人经常说假话。

Obviously, he's lying to you. Don't forget that he often lies.

18. 他去过中国的很多城市。<u>例如</u>上海、北京、广州、西安等。

He has been to many cities of China , such as Shanghai, Beijing, Guangzhou, Xi'an, etc.

19. 北京的冬天比较<u>干燥</u>，你可以买个加湿器，给房间<u>增加</u>点儿湿度。

It's rather dry in Beijing in winter. You'd better buy a humidifier to increase the humidity in the room.

20. 他爸爸脾气很<u>急躁</u>，有时候一发脾气就打他。

His father was hot-tempered. He used to give him a beating when he lost his temper.

21. <u>实际</u>上，这些都是他爷爷留下来的<u>遗产</u>。

In fact, all these are legacies handed down by his grandpa.

22. 我们的家庭<u>始终</u>充满了欢乐。

Our family is full of happiness and joy all the time.

23. 他<u>曾经</u>是我的<u>邻居</u>，后来搬走了。

He used to be my neighbour, and he moved out later.

24. 那个<u>导游</u>的普通话说得很<u>标准</u>。

The tourist guide speaks standard *putonghua*.

25. 通过<u>实践</u>，我找到了一些学习汉语的好方法。

I found some good methods of learning Chinese in practice.

26. 你这个<u>笨蛋</u>，做事总是<u>笨手笨脚</u>的。

Your fingers are all thumbs.

27. 阿里的房间在那边，我可以领你去。
    Ali's room is over there. I can take you to it.

28. 热烈欢迎新同学。
    Warmly welcome the new students.

29. 这一片树林大概有五十英亩。
    This wood covers probably 50 acres of land.

30. 这两年，来这儿学习的留学生有增无减。
    During the past two years the number of the overseas students has al-
    ways been increasing.

自学园地

Corner for Self-study

一 给下列词语注音

Mark the following words with phonetic symbols.

热烈	年龄	噪音	总统	曾经
( )	( )	( )	( )	( )
领导	邻居	增加	充满	显然
( )	( )	( )	( )	( )

二 写出本课含有下列偏旁的汉字并注音

Write out the characters with the following elements in this lesson, and
mark them with phonetic symbols.

口：_____（   ）   _____（   ）   _____（   ）

纟：_____（   ）   _____（   ）   _____（   ）

灬：_____（   ）   _____（   ）

扌：_____（   ）   _____（   ）

⺮：_____（   ）   _____（   ）

足：_____（   ）   _____（   ）

三　根据意思把左右两栏用线连起来

Link the word in the left column with the one in the right column that matches it in meaning.

睁开　　　　人数　　　　　　　　急躁的　　　　变化
减少　　　　眼睛　　　　　　　　异常的　　　　效果
增加　　　　例子　　　　　　　　干燥的　　　　目标
充满　　　　产量　　　　　　　　满意的　　　　遗产
举出　　　　希望　　　　　　　　远大的　　　　气候
节省　　　　时间　　　　　　　　丰富的　　　　脾气

四　选译填空

Choose the right characters to fill in the blanks.

1. 在这黑黑的晚上,他忽然在我身后大____了一声,____得我一身汗。

    (减、喊、感)(虾、吓)

2. 我可以给大家举个____子,来更好地说明这个问题。　　　(列、烈、例)

3. 他们的____导看上去年____有五十岁左右。　　　(零、邻、龄、领)

4. 这次语言实____活动,要求每个人都参加。　　　(贱、浅、线、践)

5. 这几天他的表现有些____常,____然是发生了什么事。　　(导、异)(温、显、湿)

6. 他们厂生产的产品已经达到了国____ ____准。　　　(标、际)

五　阅读下列句子并回答问题

Read the following sentences and answer the questions accordingly.

1. 这种药品有效期快到了,你们不应该卖了。

    这种药为什么不能卖了?

2. 中国有名的一句老话,叫做"远亲不如近邻"。

    你知道这句话的意思吗?

3. 有关这个问题,在昨天的会议上,大家进行了激烈的讨论,但意见始终没有得到统一。

    对这个问题,他们的看法一样吗?

4. 吃了这种减肥药,体重不但没有减轻,反而(on the contrary)还增加了,真是怪事。这种减肥药有效吗?

5. 他们在那片沙漠里转来转去,却始终找不到回来的路线。
   他们怎么了?

6. 昨天国家领导人在经济工作会议上指出,今年的国民经济发展要实现百分之八的经济增长目标,新华社全文报导了这位领导人的讲话。
   今年经济工作的目标是什么?

7. 在北京,有个首都钢铁厂的工人叫大刚,他收集(collect)了首都各大医院专家的信息,创办了一条以他的名字命名的电话热线——"大刚热线",专门为那些病人服务。
   大刚为什么要创办"大刚热线"?

8. 请看下列这条标语:高高兴兴上班来,平平安安回家去。
   这是一条关于什么内容的标语? 在你的国家有这样的标语吗? 请举一例。

9. 现在出现很多新词,例如:白领、蓝领、黑领、粉领、金领等,你知道这些词的意思吗? 其实,白领是指那些从事(go in for)脑力劳动(labour)的人,他们的工作环境好,可以穿白衬衣上班;蓝领是指那些从事生产、服务等体力劳动的人,他们工作时一般穿蓝色工作服;粉领是指那些从事秘书(mìshū , secretary)、打字员、会计(kuàijì ,accounting)或一些服务性职业的女子,她们穿着(zhuó)很漂亮;金领是指那些高级知识阶层或高级管理(guǎnlǐ, manage)人员,他们的收入(income)一般比较高;而黑领是指那些从事脏、累或不体面(dignity)工作的人。
   "金领"是什么人? 为什么把他们称为"金领"?

10. 这是他作为总统发表的最后演讲,标志着他四年总统任期的结束。
    这次演讲标志着什么?

第十一课

汉字园地

Corner for Chinese Characters

1.	扁	biǎn	flat
	扁平	biǎnpíng	flat
2.	编	biān	compose
	改编	gǎibiān	revise
3.	燃	rán	burn
	燃烧	ránshāo	combustion
4.	歉	qiàn	apology
	向……道歉	xiàng…dàoqiàn	apologize to
5.	姥	lǎo	
	姥姥	lǎolao	maternal grandmother
	姥爷	lǎoye	maternal grandfather
6.	匆	cōng	hurriedly
	匆忙	cōngmáng	in a hurry
7.	葱	cōng	onion
	洋葱	yángcōng	onion
8.	扣	kòu	button up
	扣子	kòuzi	button
9.	攻	gōng	attack
	进攻	jìngōng	attack
10.	巩	gǒng	consolidate
	巩固	gǒnggù	consolidate; solidify

11. 贡	gòng	tribute
贡献	gòngxiàn	contribute；contribution
12. 皮	pí	skin
皮肤	pífū	skin
13. 披	pī	drape over one's shoulders
披露	pīlù	reveal
14. 疲	pí	tired
疲劳	píláo	fatigue
15. 卷	①juǎn	roll up；fold
卷起来	juǎn qǐlai	fold
胶卷	jiāojuǎn	roll film
	②juàn	examination paper
试卷	shìjuàn	exam paper
答卷	dájuàn	answered test paper
16. 圈	quān	circle
圆圈	yuánquān	circle
17. 蠢	chǔn	foolish
愚蠢	yúchǔn	foolishness
18. 反	fǎn	oppose；turn over
反对	fǎnduì	oppose
相反	xiāngfǎn	opposite
反而	fǎn'ér	instead
反复	fǎnfù	repeatedly；relapse
反正	fǎnzhèng	anyway
19. 朵	duǒ	a measure word for flowers，clouds，etc
花朵	huāduǒ	flower
20. 巴	bā	look forward to
巴不得	bābude	eagerly look forward to
21. 求	qiú	ask；beg
要求	yāoqiú	ask；demand
请求	qǐngqiú	request
22. 秒	miǎo	second
一秒钟	yì miǎo zhōng	one second

23. 妙	miào	wonderful
巧妙	qiǎomiào	ingenious
美妙	měimiào	wonderful
24. 秘	mì	secret
秘书	mìshū	secretary
秘密	mìmì	secret
25. 密	mì	mystery; dense
密切	mìqiè	close; build close links
密码	mìmǎ	password
26. 蜜	mì	honey
蜜月	mìyuè	honeymoon
27. 蜂	fēng	bee
蜜蜂	mìfēng	bee
28. 峰	fēng	peak
山峰	shānfēng	mountain peak
峰会	fēnghuì	summit
29. 犯	fàn	violate
犯错误	fàn cuòwù	make a mistake
犯法	fànfǎ	violate the law
30. 范	fàn	model
范围	fànwéi	scope range
31. 愚	yú	foolish
愚人节	Yúrén Jié	April Fools' Day
32. 怜	lián	pity
可怜	kělián	pathetic
33. 突	tū	sudden
突然	tūrán	suddenly
突出	tūchū	highlight; outstanding
34. 献	xiàn	dedicate
献身	xiàn shēn	devote oneself to
35. 啊	ā	ah
36. 嗯	ńg	eh
37. 呐	na	
38. 嘛	ma	

记忆窍门

Tips for Memorizing Work

一 形声字声旁记忆

Memorize the following characters with the given phonetic elements.

扁 biǎn

（ˇ） 扁 flat 扁平 biǎnpíng flat

（ˉ） 编 compose 改编 gǎibiān revise

然 rán

（ ） 然 _____

（ˊ） 燃 burn 燃烧 ránshāo combustion

欠 qiàn

（ ） 欠 _____

（ˋ） 歉 apology 向……道歉 xiàng…dàoqiàn apologize to

老 lǎo

（ˇ） 姥 姥姥 lǎolao maternal grandmother

姥爷 lǎoye maternal grandfather

匆 cōng

（ˉ） 匆 hurriedly 匆忙 cōngmáng in a hurry

（ˉ） 葱 onion 洋葱 yángcōng onion

口 kǒu

（ˋ） 扣 button up 扣子 kòuzi button

工 gōng

（ ） 功 _____

（ˉ） 攻 attack 进攻 jìngōng attack

（ˇ）	巩	consolidate			
			巩固	gǒnggù	consolidate；solidify
（ˋ）	贡	tribute	贡献	gòngxiàn	contribution；contribute
（ ）	空	_____			
（ ）	红	_____			

皮　pí

（ˊ）	皮	skin	皮肤	pífū	skin
（ˉ）	披	drape over one's shoulders			
			披露	pīlù	reveal
（ˊ）	疲	tired	疲劳	píláo	fatigue

卷　juǎn/juàn

（ˇ）	卷	roll up；fold			
			卷起来	juǎn qǐlai	fold
			胶卷	jiāojuǎn	roll film
（ˋ）	卷	examination paper			
			试卷	shìjuàn	exam paper
			答卷	dájuàn	answered test paper
（quān）	圈	circle	圆圈	yuánquān	circle

春　chūn

（ ）	春	_____			
（ˇ）	蠢	foolish	愚蠢	yúchǔn	foolishness

反　fǎn

（ ）	饭	_____			
（ˇ）	反	oppose；turn over			
			反对	fǎnduì	oppose
			相反	xiāngfǎn	opposite
			反而	fǎn'ér	instead
			反复	fǎnfù	repeatedly；relapse
			反正	fǎnzhèng	anyway

朵　duǒ

（　）躲　_____

（ˇ）朵　a measure word for flowers, clouds, etc.

　　　　　　花朵　huāduǒ　　　　　flower

巴　bā

（　）把　_____

（　）吧　_____

（　）爸　_____

（ˉ）巴　look forward to

　　　　　　巴不得　bābude　　　　eagerly look forward to

求　qiú

（　）球　_____

（ˊ）求　ask；beg　请求　qǐngqiú　　　　request

　　　　　　　　　　要求　yāoqiú　　　　ask；demand

扁	编	燃	歉	姥	匆	葱	扣	攻	巩	贡	皮	披	疲

卷	圈	蠢	反	朵	巴	求

二　比较下列形近字

Compare the following characters with similar pictographic elements.

秒——妙

　　秒 miǎo　second　一秒钟 yì miǎo zhōng　one second
　　妙 miào　wonderful 巧妙　qiǎomiào　　　ingenious
　　　　　　　　　　美妙　měimiào　　　wonderful

秘——密——蜜

　　秘　mì　secret　秘书　mìshū　　　　secretary
　　　　　　　　　　秘密　mìmì　　　　secret
　　密　mì　mystery；dense
　　　　　　　　　　密切　mìqiè　　　　close；build close links

			密码	mìmǎ	password
蜜	mì	honey	蜜月	mìyuè	honeymoon

蜂——峰

蜂	fēng	bee	蜜蜂	mìfēng	bee
峰	fēng	peak	山峰	shānfēng	mountain peak
			峰会	fēnghuì	summit

犯——范

犯	fàn	violate	犯错误	fàn cuòwù	make a mistake
			犯法	fàn fǎ	violate the law
范	fàn		范围	fànwéi	scope range

寓——遇——愚

寓	_____
遇	_____
愚	yú	foolish	愚人节	Yúrén Jié	April Fools' Day

邻——怜

邻	_____
怜	lián	pity	可怜	kělián	pathetic

秒	妙	秘	密	蜜	蜂	峰	犯	范	愚	怜

三　形声字形旁记忆

Memorize the following characters with the given pictographic elements.

犬——突　tū　sudden　突然　tūrán　　　suddenly
　　　　　　　　　　突出　tūchū　　　highlight, outstanding
　　献　xiàn　dedicate
　　　　　　　　　　献身　xiàn shēn　devote oneself to

口——啊　ā　ah; oh (expressing surprise or amazement)
　　　　　啊，他跑得真快呀！ Oh, see how fast he runs!
　　　á　(pressing for an answer or asking for something to be repeated)
　　　　　啊？你明天到底去不去呀！
　　　　　Well, are you going tomorrow or not?

ǎ　(indicating surprise and doubt)

啊？这是怎么回事？Ah，what is going on?

à　(expressing sudden realization or agreement)

啊，原来是你，怪不得看着面熟呢！

Ah，so it's you! Small wonder you look so familiar.

a　(used at the end of a sentence to indicate admiration and to ment on sb.)

你可要小心啊！Do be careful!

嗯　ńg　(used for having words repeated when not heard)

嗯，你说什么？Eh，what did you say?

ňg　(indicating surprise or disapproval)

嗯！你怎么还没去？Hey，haven't you gone yet?

ǹg　(indicating a reply)

他"嗯"了一声就走了。

He muttered an 'Uhhuh', and went away.

呐　na　(equivalent to"啊")

谢谢你呐。Thanks a lot.

嘛　ma　(indicating that sth. is obvious)

这样做就是不对嘛！Of course it was acting improperly!

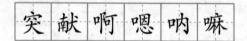

活用园地

Corner for Flexible Usage

Form words and phrases.

扁　扁豆　bean　扁圆　oblate　扁盒子　crushed box

编　编号　number　编制　work out　主编　editor in chief

邮政编码　postal code

燃	点燃　light (a fire)　燃料　fuel
歉	歉意　apology
葱	大葱　green Chinese onion　小葱　spring onion
扣	扣留　detain　扣住　cover　扣除　deduct
	回扣　sales commission
攻	围攻　attack from all sides　快攻　quick attack
	反攻　counteroffensive　攻读　assiduously study
	攻关　storm a strategic pass　攻击　capture
皮	树皮　bark　土豆皮　potato peel　香蕉皮　banana skin
	皮大衣　fur coat　皮带　leather belt　皮球　rubber ball
	皮鞋　leather shoes　皮箱　leather suitcase
披	披风　cloak　披肩　cape　披头散发　with hair dishevelled
疲	疲乏　tired　疲软　fatigued and weak
卷	①juǎn
	花卷　steamed roll
	②juàn
	画卷　scroll　开卷　open exam
圈	圈子　circle　圈套　trap
蠢	蠢货　idiot　蠢话　nonsense　蠢事　stupidity
反	反常　unusual　反感　disgusted with (sb. or sth.)
	反过来　conversely　反面　back；opposite　反义　antonym
	反应　respond；response　反动　reactionary
朵	一朵花　a flower　一朵云　a cloud
巴	尾巴　tail　下巴　chin　嘴巴　mouth
求	需求　demand　追求　seek　求爱　court　求婚　propose
	求情　plead　求之不得　most welcome
秒	分秒　every minute and second　秒表　stop watch
	分秒必争　seize every minute and second
妙	巧妙　ingenious　奇妙　wonderful　妙计　wise tactic
秘	秘书　secretary　秘史　secret history
密	紧密　closely　亲密　close　哈密瓜　a kind of muskmelon grown in Hami，Xinjiang Autonomous Region，China
蜜	水蜜桃　honey peach　花蜜　nectar

蜂	蜂蜜 honey	蜂群 bee colony

蜂　蜂蜜　honey　蜂群　bee colony
峰　高峰　summit　主峰　main peak　险峰　dangerous peaks
犯　犯病　get ill　犯法　violate the law　犯规　break the rule
　　犯人　convict　主犯　chief criminal　违犯　violate
范　典范　model　示范　demonstrate　规范　rules and regulations
　　师范　normal school
愚　愚人　fool　愚笨　dull-witted；stupid　愚弄　deceive
怜　爱怜　love with pity　怜惜　take pity for
　　同病相怜　fellow sufferers commiserate with one another
突　突击　sudden attack　冲突　conflict　突破　break through
　　突如其来　come all of a sudden

二　认读句子

Read and try to understand the following sentences.

1. 那盘磁带放在那个扁平的盒子里了。
The tape was put in that flat box.

2. 这个电影是根据他的小说改编的。
This film is adapted from his novel.

3. 这场森林大火很大，一直燃烧了两个多月。
The forest fire spread to a large area and lasted over two months.

4. 这件毛衣的扣子真漂亮。
The woolen sweater has beautiful buttons.

5. 敌人开始进攻了。
The enemy has started their attack.

6. 要不断复习才能巩固学到的知识。
We should constantly go over the knowledge that we have learned so as to consolidate it.

7. 努力学习，为自己的国家多作贡献。
Study hard and dedicate yourselves to the country.

8. 天冷了，披件衣服再出去散步吧。
It's getting cold. Put on some more before you go out for a walk.

9. 昨天我太疲劳了，晚上一躺下就睡着了。
I was so tired that I fell asleep immediately once I lay on my bed.

10. 那个孩子把手中的花<u>献</u>给了老师。

The child presented the flowers in his hand to his teacher.

11. 今天一百米他跑了十一<u>秒</u>六。

He finished the one-hundred-meter dash in 11.6 seconds today.

12. 这是我的<u>秘密</u>,你一定为我<u>保</u>密。

This is my secret, and you must keep it to youself.

13. 结婚以后他们俩要去国外度<u>蜜月</u>。

After their wedding, they are going abroad to spend their honeymoon.

14. 他在一家电脑公司做<u>秘书</u>工作。

She is working with a computer company as a secretary.

15. 每个人都可能<u>犯</u>错误。

To err is human.

16. 他的心脏病又<u>犯</u>了。

He had another heart attack.

17. 不论你怎么说,反正你这样做太<u>愚蠢</u>了。

I think it was too foolish of you to have done so.

18. 你看那个孩子哭得多<u>可怜</u>啊!

Look, how pathetic that weeping boy is!

19. 你别当真,他是在跟你开玩笑呢,因为今天是<u>愚人</u>节。

Don't take it seriously. He was only joking with you because it's April Fools' Day today.

20. 他的父母以前一直同意他跟女朋友结婚,现在不知道为什么突然开始<u>反对</u>起来了。

His parents have been approving of his marriage with his girl friend, and he doesn't know why they begin to oppose it now.

21. 老板<u>要求</u>他下午就出差到广州,他愉快地接受了。

The boss asked him to go on a business trip to Guangzhou this after-noon, and he accepted.

22. 喂,你大声一点儿,我年纪大了,<u>耳朵</u>不好,听不清你在说什么。

Hey, speak louder, please. Otherwise I can not hear you because I'm old and my hearing is not so good.

23. 后天不用去上海出差了,太好了,我正<u>巴不得</u>,本来我家里事就多,我爱人也不在家,我根本就走不开。

I needn't go on a trip to Shanghai the day after tomorrow. That's great! I have wished so. A lot of things have happened to my family and my wife is not in. So I can not leave at all.

24. <u>姥姥</u>就是妈妈的妈妈。

"姥姥"is the mother of one's mother.

25. 他已经为他昨天<u>愚蠢</u>的行为反复地向你<u>道了歉</u>，你就别再生气了。

He has apologized repeatedly to you for his stupid behavior. Please don't be angry and longer.

26. 这个灯设计得很<u>巧妙</u>。

This light is an ingenious device.

27. 我把信用卡的<u>密码</u>忘了，刷不了卡了。

I have forgot the password of my credit card and I can't punch it.

28. 孩子是祖国的<u>花朵</u>。

Children are the flowers of our country.

29. 珠穆朗玛峰是世界最高<u>山峰</u>，高八千多米。

Mount Qomolangma, the highest peak in the world, is over 8,000 meters.

30. 你向别的公司<u>披露</u>了我们的商业<u>秘密</u>，这样做是<u>犯法</u>的。

You have revealed our business secret to other companies. That is against the law.

自学园地
Corner for Self-study

一 给下列词语注音

Mark the following words with phonetic symbols.

美妙　　　　贡献　　　　疲劳　　　　可怜　　　　突然
（　　　）（　　　）（　　　）（　　　）（　　　）

秘书　　　　密码　　　　相反　　　　燃烧　　　　道歉
（　　　）（　　　）（　　　）（　　　）（　　　）

二 组词

Form words and phrases.

求：_____　_____　　　　妙：_____　_____

突：_____　_____　　　　犯：_____　_____

密：_____　_____　　　　反：_____　_____

皮：_____　_____　　　　愚：_____　_____

三　根据意思把左右两栏用线连起来

Link the word in the left column with the one in the right column that matches it in meaning.

巩固	中心		美妙的	花朵
提出	秘密		高大的	贡献
发现	请求		相反的	范围
贡献	知识		美丽的	山峰
突出	小说		复习的	结果
改编	力量		伟大的	音乐

四　选择填空

Choose the right characters to fill in the blanks.

1. 他们俩关系一直很_____切。　　　　　　　　　　（密、蜜）
2. 他太_____劳了，坐在沙发上睡着了。　　　　　　（披、疲）
3. 这个主意_____极了！　　　　　　　　　　　　　（秒、妙）
4. 这些课本都是由他_____写的。　　　　　　　　　（偏、编、骗）
5. 这已经是他第二次_____规了，因为两张红牌，他被请出了比赛场。

（范、犯、反）

五　阅读下列句子并回答问题

Read the following sentences and answer the questions accordingly.

1. 前几年他们交往很密切，最近两年由于工作太忙，联系反而少了。

   他们现在还密切联系吗？

2. 汽车在半路上突然坏了，他想向路过的汽车司机请求帮助，可是由于太晚了，等了半天也没见一辆车来。

   他得到帮助了吗？为什么？

3. 他们是兄弟俩,虽然长得很像,性格却正好<u>相反</u>。

   他们俩性格一样吗?

4. 王教授在上课的时候注意<u>突出</u>教学中的重点和难点,因此受到了学生的普遍欢迎。

   王教授课上得怎么样?

5. 考试的<u>范围</u>、要求就讲到这儿,请大家抓紧时间复习<u>巩固</u>,争取取得好成绩。

   刚才说话人讲到了什么?

6. 哪道题做错了,就在试卷的题号上画个<u>圆圈</u>,作个标志,便于以后复习。

   老师要求在试卷上作什么标记?

7. 在昨天的亚非<u>峰会</u>上,参加会议的亚洲和非洲各国领导人就亚非经济贸易合作等问题展开了讨论。

   昨天的亚非峰会讨论了什么问题?

8. 请帮我把这些<u>胶卷</u>洗一下,这张纸上写着号码的要放大。

   说话人现在在哪儿?

9. 请大家注意,一定要把答案写在 HSK 的<u>答卷</u>上,写在<u>试卷</u>上的答案无效。

   答案能不能写在试卷上? 为什么?

10. <u>姥姥</u>、<u>姥爷</u>,公司<u>突然</u>来电话,让马上回去,这次来上海,因时间<u>匆忙</u>,来不及去看你们了,下次来我一定去看你们。

    说话人为什么没去看姥姥、姥爷?

第十二课

汉字园地
Corner for Chinese Characters

1.	格	gé	squares formed by crossed lines
	价格	jiàgé	price
	及格	jígé	passing grade
2.	恢	huī	extensive
	恢复	huīfù	get recovered
3.	尊	zūn	noble
	尊重	zūnzhòng	respect
4.	遵	zūn	follow
	遵照	zūnzhào	conform to
5.	敬	jìng	respect
	敬爱	jìng'ài	respect and love
	尊敬	zūnjìng	respect
6.	警	jǐng	alert
	警察	jǐngchá	police
	报警	bào jǐng	report to the police
7.	则	zé	rule
	原则	yuánzé	principle
	规则	guīzé	rule; regulation
8.	测	cè	survey
	测验	cèyàn	test

9. 侧	cè	side; lean
侧面	cèmiàn	side
两侧	liǎngcè	on both sides
10. 厕	cè	lavatory; toilet
厕所	cèsuǒ	lavatory; toilet; W. C.
11. 救	jiù	rescue
救人	jiù rén	save a person from danger, etc.
救命	jiù mìng	help
12. 伍	wǔ	army
队伍	duìwu	troops
13. 曹	Cáo	(a surname)
14. 遭	zāo	meet with
遭到	zāodào	meet with (misfortune)
遭受	zāoshòu	suffer
15. 兆	zhào	sign
兆头	zhàotou	sign
16. 挑	tiāo	pick
挑选	tiāoxuǎn	select
17. 跳	tiào	jump
跳舞	tiào wǔ	dance
18. 桃	táo	peach
桃子	táozi	peach
19. 逃	táo	escape
逃走	táozǒu	run away
20. 寺	sì	temple
寺庙	sìmiào	temple
21. 诗	shī	poem
诗人	shīrén	poet
诗歌	shīgē	poetry
22. 持	chí	hold
支持	zhīchí	support

23.	苗	miáo	young shoot
	苗条	miáotiao	slim
24.	庙	miào	temple
	庙会	miàohuì	fair
25.	竞	jìng	compete
	竞赛	jìngsài	contest; competition
	竞争	jìngzhēng	compete with
26.	性	xìng	sex; nature; gender
	性格	xìnggé	character
	可能性	kěnéngxìng	possibility
	急性子	jí xìngzi	quick-tempered
27.	恼	nǎo	be annoyed
	烦恼	fánnǎo	worried
28.	谅	liàng	understand
	原谅	yuánliàng	forgive
29.	保	bǎo	safeguard
	保证	bǎozhèng	guarantee
	保持	bǎochí	keep
	保护	bǎohù	protect; protection
	保留	bǎoliú	retain
	保险	bǎoxiǎn	insurance
30.	傻	shǎ	foolish
	傻瓜	shǎguā	fool
31.	伤	shāng	wound
	伤心	shāngxīn	broken-hearted
	受伤	shòushāng	get wounded
32.	劳	láo	work
	劳动	láodòng	labor
33.	劝	quàn	persuade
	劝告	quàngào	persuasion

34. 守	shǒu	guard；keep；abide by
遵守	zūnshǒu	abide by
35. 牢	láo	fast；jail；fold
牢记	láojì	remember well
牢骚	láosāo	complaint
36. 害	hài	evil；harm
害怕	hàipà	fear
害处	hàichù	harm

记忆窍门
Tips for Memorizing Work

一　形声字声旁记忆

Memorize the following characters with the given phonetic elements.

各　gè

（′）格　squares formed by crossed lines

价格　jiàgé　price

及格　jígé　passing grade

（　）客 _____

（　）路 _____

灰　huī

（　）灰 _____

（—）恢　extensive

恢复　huīfù　get recovered

尊　zūn

（—）尊　noble

尊重　zūnzhòng　respect

	（一）	遵	follow	遵照	zūnzhào	conform to

敬 jìng

（丶）	敬	respect	敬爱	jìng'ài	respect and love
			尊敬	zūnjìng	respect
（ˇ）	警	alert	警察	jǐngchá	police
			报警	bào jǐng	report to the police

则 zé

（ˊ）	则	rule	原则	yuánzé	principle
			规则	guīzé	rule
（cè）	测	survey	测验	cèyàn	test
（cè）	侧	side	侧面	cèmiàn	side
			两侧	liǎngcè	on both sides
（cè）	厕	lavatory；toilet	厕所	cèsuǒ	lavatory

求 qiú

（ ）	求	_____			
（jiù）	救	rescue	救人	jiù rén	save a person from danger, etc.
			救命	jiù mìng	help

五 wǔ

（ˇ）	伍	army	队伍	duìwǔ	troops

曹 cáo

（ ）	曹	_____			
（ ）	糟	_____			
（zāo）	遭	meet with	遭到	zāodào	meet with (misfortune)
			遭受	zāoshòu	suffer

兆 zhào

（丶）	兆	sign	兆头	zhàotou	sign
（tiāo）	挑	pick	挑选	tiāoxuǎn	select
（tiào）	跳	jump	跳舞	tiào wǔ	dance
（táo）	桃	peach	桃子	táozi	peach
（táo）	逃	escape	逃走	táozǒu	run away

寺　SÌ

(丶)	寺	temple	寺庙	sìmiào	temple
(shī)	诗	poem	诗人	shīrén	poet
			诗歌	shīgē	poetry
(chí)	持	hold	支持	zhīchí	support

格	恢	尊	遵	敬	警	则	测	侧	厕	救	伍	曹	遭
兆	挑	跳	桃	逃	寺	诗	持						

二　比较同音、近音字

Compare the following characters with same or similar pronunciation.

苗——庙

苗	miáo	young shoot	苗条 miáotiao	slim
庙	miào	temple	庙会 miàohuì	fair

竟——竞

竟 _____

竞	jìng	compete	竞赛 jìngsài	contest; competition
			竞争 jìngzhēng	compete with

星——姓——性

星 _____

姓 _____

性 xìng　sex; nature; gender

性格	xìnggé	character
可能性	kěnéngxìng	possibility
急性子	jí xìngzi	quick-tempered

脑——恼

脑 _____

恼	nǎo	be annoyed	烦恼 fánnǎo	worried

凉——谅

谅 _____

谅 liàng   understand

原谅 yuánliàng   forgive

苗	庙	竞	性	恼	谅

三 形声字形旁记忆

Memorize the following characters with the given pictographic elements.

亻——保 bǎo safegurad
保证 bǎozhèng   guarantee
保持 bǎochí   keep
保护 bǎohù   protect; protection
保留 bǎoliú   retain

傻 shǎ foolish   傻瓜 shǎguā   fool

伤 shāng wound   伤心 shāngxīn   broken-hecrted
受伤 shòu shāng   get wounded

力——劳 láo work   劳动 láodòng   labor
劝 quàn persuade   劝告 quàngào   persuasion

宀——守 shǒu guard;keep;abide by
遵守 zūnshǒu   abide by

牢 láo fast;jail   牢记 láojì   remember well
牢骚 láosāo   complaint

害 hài evil;harm   害怕 hàipà   fear
害处 hàichù   harm

保	傻	伤	劳	劝	守	牢	害

活用园地
Corner for Flexible Usage

Form words and phrases.

格	风格 style	表格 form	品格 moral character		
	规格 specification	人格 personality	合格 qualified		
	格言 maxim	格外 especially	格局 pattern	格式 format	
恢	恢复期 period for recovery				
尊	自尊 self-respect	自尊心 self-respect			
	尊姓大名 your honored name				
遵	遵从 follow	遵命 obey your command	遵照 obey		
敬	敬礼 salute	敬酒 propose a toast	敬茶 present tea		
	敬老院 old people's home				
	敬而远之 keep someone at a respectful distance				
警	警告 warn	警报 alarm	警犬 police dog	警亭 police box	
	报警 report to the police	民警 people's police	火警 fire alarm		
则	法则 law	准则 norm	简则 general regulations in brief		
	总则 general rules				
测	测试 test	测验 test	测定 survey and determine		
	测量 measure；survey	测算 measure and calculate			
	猜测 guess	预测 predict			
侧	侧身 turn sideways	侧影 profile	两侧 on both sides		
厕	公厕 public latrine	男厕所 men's room	女厕所 women's room		
救	救火 put down the fire	救命 save lives			
	救灾 provide disaster relief	急救 first aid			
	求救 ask for help	得救 be saved	呼救 call for help		
	救生衣 life jacket				
伍	入伍 join the army	退伍 be dismissed from the army			
遭	遭遇 encounter	遭到 suffer			
兆	前兆 omen	先兆 indication	预兆 sign	亿兆 mega million	

挑　①tiāo

　　挑毛病　find fault

　　②tiǎo

　　挑战　challenge

跳　跳动　beat　跳高　high jump　跳远　long jump　跳水　dive

　　跳马　vaulting horse　跳伞　parachuting　心跳　heart beat

　　心惊肉跳　frightening

逃　逃跑　escape　逃学　skip school

桃　桃花　peach flower　桃树　peach　桃红色　peach color

寺　寺院　temple　清真寺　mosque

持　持续　continue　主持　preside　持久　lasting　持平　keep balance

苗　禾苗　shoots　苗族　the Miaos

庙　庙堂　temple　太庙　the lmperial Ancestral Temple

　　一座庙　a temple

竞　竞走　heel-and-toe walking race　竞选　run for election

性　性子　disposition　性情　temperament　性急　impatient

　　性能　function　性命　life　性别　sex　本性　nature

　　人性　human nature　天性　born nature　个性　personality

　　任性　willful　记性　memory　特性　characteristics

　　男性　male　女性　female　共性　generality　慢性　chronic

　　可行性　feasibility　艺术性　artistry　必然性　necessity

　　积极性　enthusiasm

恼　恼火　irritated　气恼　annoyed　苦恼　vexed

谅　谅解　understand　体谅　show sympathetic understanding of

　　见谅　forgive

保　保安　ensure safety　保留　reserve

　　保守　conservative　保重　take care　保密　keep secret

　　保持　preserve　保护　protect　保温　heat preservation

　　保健　health protection　保养　maintenance　保姆(mǔ)　housemaid

　　保健品　health protecting food　保龄球　bowling

傻　傻子　fool　傻眼　be dumbfounded

伤　伤害　harm　伤亡　casualties　伤口　wound

　　伤员　wounded soldiers　外伤　exterior wound

　　重伤　heavily wounded　负伤　be wounded

劳	劳累 fatigue 劳驾 excuse me 功劳 contribution
	劳动力 labour 劳动节 Labor Day
劝	劝说 persuade 劝酒 urge someone to drink
守	保守 conservative 守法 law-abiding 守信用 keep one's promise
牢	坐牢 be in jail 牢固 firm
害	害虫 insect 害处 disadvantage 利害 gains and losses
	伤害 harm 有害 harmful 无害 harmless
	受害 be a victim of 灾害 calamity

二 认读句子

Read and try to understand the following sentences.

1. 真糟糕，这次测验我又没及格。
   What bad luck! I failed the exam again.

2. 祝你早日恢复健康。
   Wish you a speedy recovery.

3. 孩子们都很尊重他们的老师。
   The children have respect for their teachers.

4. 遵照学校的规定，缺课太多就不能参加考试了。
   According to the school's rules, those who have missed too many of the classes are not allowed to sit in for exams.

5. 大家都应该尊敬老人。
   Everybody should show respect to the seniors.

6. 为了您和他人的安全，请遵守交通规则。
   For your safety and others', please abide by traffic rules.

7. 从侧面看，他很像他哥哥。
   If you look at his profile, he resembles his brother.

8. 请问，附近有厕所吗？
   Excuse me, is there a lavatory around?

9. 一九九八年，中国很多地方都遭受了水灾。
   Many places in China suffered from flooded in 1998.

10. 他高兴得跳了起来。
    He jumped with joy.

11. 那个司机不仅不救人，反而驾车逃走了，现在警察正在追查他。
    Instead of helping the person he had hit, the driver drove away. And now

the police are after him.

12. 他是个有名的诗人,写了很多深受大家喜爱的诗歌。

He's a well-known poet, who has written a lot of poems best loved by the populace.

13. 我想,你的意见是对的,我支持你。

I think your idea is correct and I'm behind you.

14. 现在的年轻人,特别是女孩子,都追求苗条,很多人都想减肥。

Nowadays many young people, especially girls, seek slimness and want to go on a diet.

15. 每年二月,这儿都有庙会,非常热闹。

There's a fair with a lot of excitement here in February every year.

16. 这一条街饭店很多,竞争也很激烈。

There are lots of restaurants in this street and competition is fierce.

17. 那个有名的寺庙就建在前面的山峰上。

The famous temple was built on top of the hill in front.

18. 请原谅,我来晚了。

Please forgive me for being late.

19. 在那次足球比赛中,他的腿受了伤。

He got his leg hurt in the football match.

20. 你这样做太傻了。我劝你别去,你不听。

It's most silly of you to do so. I tried to persuade you not to go, but you would not listen to me.

21. 学过的东西,他总是记得很牢。

He always remembers well whatever he has learned.

22. 他很害怕他爸爸发脾气。

He will be frightened when his father loses his temper.

23. 今天是我女朋友的生日,请你给我挑一个最漂亮的蛋糕。

Today is my girlfriend's birthday. Please choose the most beautiful cake for me.

24. 因为他们几个汉语说得比较好,电视台要挑选他们去参加晚会。

As they speak fairly good Chinese, the TV station will select them for the party.

25. 我可以请你跳个舞吗?

Can I invite you to dance?

26. 我很喜欢吃水果,苹果、梨、桃子、香蕉等我都喜欢。

I like fruit, and apples, pears, peaches and bananas are all my favorites.

27. 他一发现家被偷了,就打110电话报了警,警察十分钟之内就到了现场。

He dialed 110 to report to the police once he had found that his house was burgled. And the police reached the scene within 10 minutes.

28. 他很迷信,觉得眼皮(yǎnpí)跳就不是个好兆头。

He is rather superstitious. He feels it a bad omen when his eyes keep twitching.

29. 五一劳动节休息三天。

We have three days off for May Day, the Labor Day.

30. 他根本就不听我的劝告。

He won't accept my advice.

自学园地

Corner for Self-study

一 **给下列词语注音**

Mark the following words with phonetic symbols.

原谅　　　　傻瓜　　　　害怕　　　　劳动　　　　原则

(　　　　)　(　　　　)　(　　　　)　(　　　　)　(　　　　)

报警　　　　尊敬　　　　苗条　　　　厕所　　　　跳舞

(　　　　)　(　　　　)　(　　　　)　(　　　　)　(　　　　)

二 **写出本课含有下列偏旁的汉字并注音**

Write out the characters with the following elements in this lesson, and mark them with phonetic symbols.

亻:_____(　　)　　_____(　　)　　_____(　　)　　_____(　　)

　　_____(　　)

辶:_____(　　)　　_____(　　)　　_____(　　)　　_____(　　)

忄:_____(　　)　　_____(　　)　　_____(　　)

宀:_____(　　)　　_____(　　)　　_____(　　)

女:_____(　　)　　_____(　　)

木:_____(　　)　　_____(　　)

三 根据意思把左右两栏用线连起来

Link the word in the left column with the one in the right column that matches it in meaning.

古怪的   价格   热闹的   规则

便宜的   庙会   成功的   厕所

竞赛的   性格   敬爱的   害处

洁静的   可能性   吸烟的   老师

四 选词填空

Choose the right words to fill in the blanks.

尊重   尊敬   敬爱   热爱

1. 父母应该_____孩子的选择。

2. _____书吧，它是我们的朋友。

3. 我的父亲是我最_____的人。

4. 警察的工作虽然很辛苦，但是他们得到了人们普遍的_____。

遵守   遵照

1. 我们是_____董事长的指示办事。

2. 大家都应该_____保险合同嘛，你们这样做不是违约吗？

受到   遭受

1. 这种病使他_____了极大的痛苦。

2. 这种桌子设计巧妙，_____了大家的欢迎。

保护   保持

1. 毕业十多年了，他们始终_____着密切的联系。

2. 他们成立了一个_____野生动物的小组。

竞争   竞赛

1. 现在的大学生毕业以后找到一个好工作也不容易，_____很激烈。

2. 这两个工厂的工人正在开展劳动_____。

五　阅读下列句子并回答问题

Read the following sentences and answer the questions accordingly.

1. 妻子是个<u>急性子</u>,而丈夫却是个<u>慢性子</u>,有时候丈夫的"慢慢来"能把妻子气哭了。

   妻子为什么哭?

2. 我真不明白,吸烟的<u>害处</u>大家都知道,但还是有那么多人吸。

   "我"不明白什么?

3. 学习汉语应该<u>遵守</u>先易后难的<u>原则</u>。

   应该怎么学汉语?

4. <u>敬爱</u>的<u>曹</u>教授,最近因为出国,没有及时给您回信,请您<u>原谅</u>。

   说话人为什么要请曹教授原谅?

5. 这个城市很有意思,马路<u>两侧</u>都种满了<u>桃树</u>,春天<u>桃花</u>开的时候吸引着很多游客。

   为什么游客喜欢春天去那儿?

6. 去年,汽车的<u>价格</u>有所下降,但今年初,因为需求量的增加,<u>价格</u>又恢复到了原来的水平。

   从去年到现在,汽车价格有什么样的变化?

7. 保护环境,人人有责。

   这句话是什么意思?

8. 我真希望现在走进来的这支<u>队伍</u>能赢得这次<u>竞赛</u>,但我知道,这种<u>可能性</u>很小。

   这支队伍能不能赢得竞赛?

9. 您好,打扰了,我是<u>保险</u>公司的工作人员,我们公司今年又新增加了一种人身<u>伤害险</u>,我们上门给你作一个介绍,看看你是不是需要参加这个<u>保险</u>。

   说话人在做什么?

10. 昨天你说的那<u>些</u>傻话太伤她的<u>心</u>了,我<u>劝</u>了她半天,她还是不肯原谅你。

    她为什么不肯原谅"你"?

第十三课

汉字园地
Corner for Chinese Characters

1.	逗	dòu	stay
	逗留	dòuliú	linger
2.	露	①lù	reveal
	露天	lùtiān	in the open
		②lòu	show
	露面	lòu miàn	put in an appearance
3.	缩	suō	shrink
	缩小	suōxiǎo	shrink
4.	束	shù	tie
	结束	jiéshù	put an end to; come to an end
5.	速	sù	speedy
	速度	sùdù	speed
	高速公路	gāosù gōnglù	freeway
6.	剧	jù	play
	剧场	jùchǎng	theatre
	话剧	huàjù	play
	京剧	jīngjù	Beijing opera
7.	据	jù	according to; proof
	根据	gēnjù	according to
	据说	jùshuō	it's said that

8.	壮	zhuàng	strong;strengthen
	强壮	qiángzhuàng	strong
9.	装	zhuāng	act as;hold;clothing
	假装	jiǎzhuāng	pretend to be/do
	服装	fúzhuāng	clothing
	包装	bāozhuāng	pack;package
10.	当	dāng	work as;just as;should
	当然	dāngrán	of course
	当……的时候	dāng…de shíhou	when...
	当地	dāngdì	local
	当时	dāngshí	at that time
	当年	dāngnián	in those years
	相当	xiāngdāng	equal
11.	挡	dǎng	stop;block
	挡住	dǎngzhù	stop
12.	固	gù	firm
	固定	gùdìng	fix
13.	占	zhàn	occupy;constitute
	占多数	zhàn duōshù	constitute the majority
14.	战	zhàn	fight
	战争	zhànzhēng	war
	战胜	zhànshèng	defeat
15.	抱	bào	hold in one's arms;cherish
	抱歉	bàoqiàn	apologize
16.	幻	huàn	imagine
	幻想	huànxiǎng	fantasy
17.	幼	yòu	young
	幼儿园	yòu'éryuán	kindergarten
18.	它	tā	it
	它们	tāmen	they or them

19. 宅	zhái	house
住宅	zhùzhái	residence
20. 闭	bì	close
倒闭	dǎobì	close down
21. 闲	xián	leisure
休闲	xiūxián	leisure
空闲	kòngxián	be free
22. 予	yǔ	give
给予	jǐyǔ	give; render
23. 矛	máo	spear
矛盾	máodùn	contradiction
24. 盾	dùn	shield
自相矛盾	zì xiāng máodùn	be self-contradictory
25. 质	zhì	quality
质量	zhìliàng	quality
性质	xìngzhì	nature
26. 压	yā	press
压力	yālì	pressure
27. 厌	yàn	be tired of
讨厌	tǎoyàn	dislike
28. 击	jī	beat
拳击	quánjī	boxing
29. 即	jí	be; immediately
立即	lìjí	at once
即使……也	jíshǐ…yě	even if
30. 状	zhuàng	shape; condition
状况	zhuàngkuàng	situation
状态	zhuàngtài	state
31. 碎	suì	broken
打碎	dǎsuì	break
32. 强	qiáng	strong; better
强大	qiángdà	strong and powerful

加强	jiāqiáng	strengthen
强调	qiángdiào	emphasize
33. 暗	àn	dark；hidden
黑暗	hēi'àn	darkness
34. 戏	xì	drama
戏剧	xìjù	drama
游戏	yóuxì	game
35. 移	yí	move
移动	yídòng	move
36. 量	liàng	quantity
大量	dàliàng	a large quantity of
重量	zhòngliàng	weight
力量	lìliàng	power
产量	chǎnliàng	output
37. 顺	shùn	smooth
顺利	shùnlì	smooth
顺便	shùnbiàn	incidentally
38. 废	fèi	waste
废品	fèipǐn	waste
废话	fèihuà	nonsense

记忆窍门

Tips for Memorizing Work

一 形声字声旁记忆

Memorize the following characters with the given phonetic elements.

豆   dòu

（ ）豆 _____

（ ` ）逗 stay   逗留 dòuliú   linger

路　lù

　　（　）　路　_____

　　（丶）　露　reveal　露天　lùtiān　　　　in the open

　　（lòu）露　show　　露面　lòu miàn　　put in an appearance

宿　sù

　　（　）　宿　_____

　　（suō）缩　shrink　缩小　suōxiǎo　　　shrink

束　shù

　　（丶）　束　tie　　　结束　jiéshù　　　come to an end；put an end to

　　（sù）　速　speedy　速度　sùdù　　　　speed

　　　　　　　　　　高速公路　gāosù gōnglù　　freeway

居　jū

　　（　）　居　_____

　　（丶）　剧　play　　剧场　jùchǎng　　theatre

　　　　　　　　　　话剧　huàjù　　　　play

　　　　　　　　　　京剧　jīngjù　　　　Beijing opera

　　（丶）　据　according to；proof

　　　　　　　　　　根据　gēnjù　　　　according to

　　　　　　　　　　据说　jùshuō　　　　it's said that...

壮　zhuàng

　　（丶）　壮　strong；strengthen

　　　　　　　　　　强壮　qiángzhuàng　strong

　　（一）　装　act as；hold；clothing

　　　　　　　　　　假装　jiǎzhuāng　　pretend to do/be

　　　　　　　　　　服装　fúzhuāng　　clothing

　　　　　　　　　　包装　bāozhuāng　　pack；package

当　dāng

　　（一）　当

　　　　　　　　　　当然　dāngrán　　　of course

　　　　　　　　　　当……的时候　dāng...de shíhou　when...

　　　　　　　　　　当地　dāngdì　　　　local

	当时	dāngshí	at that time
	当年	dāngnián	in those years
	相当	xiāngdāng	equal

（ˇ）挡　stop；block

当　当时　dāngshí　at that time

挡住　dǎngzhù　stop

古　gǔ

（　）估　_____

（　）姑　_____

（　）故　_____

（ˋ）固　firm　　固定　gùdìng　　fix

（　）苦　_____

占　zhàn

（　）站　_____

（ˋ）占　occupy；constitute

占多数　zhàn duōshù　constitute the majority

（ˋ）战　fight

战争　zhànzhēng　war

战胜　zhànshèng　defeat

包　bāo

（　）饱　_____

（ˋ）抱　hold in one's arms；cherish

抱歉　bàoqiàn　apologize

逗	露	缩	束	速	剧	据	壮	装	当	挡	固	占	战	抱

二　比较下列形近字

Compare the following characters with similar pictographic elements.

幻——幼

幻　huàn　imagine　　幻想　huànxiǎng　　fantasy

幼　yòu　young　　幼儿园　yòu'éryuán　kindergarten

它——宅

它	tā	it	它们	tāmen	they or them
宅	zhái	house	住宅	zhùzhái	residence

闭——闲

闭	bì	close	倒闭	dǎobì	close down
闲	xián	leisure	休闲	xiūxián	leisure
			空闲	kòngxián	be free

予——矛

予	yǔ	give	给予	jǐyǔ	give
矛	máo	spear	矛盾	máodùn	contradiction

盾——质

盾	dùn	shield	自相矛盾	zì xiāng máodùn	be self-contradictory
质	zhì	quality	质量	zhìliàng	quality
			性质	xìngzhì	nature

压——厌

压	yā	press	压力	yālì	pressure
厌	yàn	be tired of	讨厌	tǎoyàn	dislike

出——击

出					
击	jī	beat	拳击	quánjī	boxing

既——即

既					
即	jí	be;immediately	立即	lìjí	at once
			即使……也……	jíshǐ…yě…	even if

壮——状

壮	zhuàng	strong;strengthen			
			强壮	qiángzhuàng	strong
状	zhuàng	shape;condition			
			状况	zhuàngkuàng	situation
			状态	zhuàngtài	state

醉──碎

醉

碎 suì broken   打碎 dǎsuì   break

幻	幼	它	宅	闭	闲	予	矛	盾	质	压	厌	击	即

壮	状	碎

三 部件构字

Memorize the following characters formed by the given parts.

弓
虽

强 qiáng

强大 qiángdà   powerful and strong
加强 jiāqiáng   strengthen
强调 qiángdiào   emphasize

日
音

暗 àn

黑暗 hēi'àn   darkness

又
戈

戏 xì

戏剧 xìjù   drama
游戏 yóuxì   game

禾
多

移 yí

移动 yídòng   move

曰
一
里

量 liàng

大量 dàliàng   a large quantity of
重量 zhòngliàng   weight
力量 lìliàng   power, strength
产量 chǎnliàng   output

川
页

顺 shùn

顺利 shùnlì   smooth
顺便 shùnbiàn   incidentally

废 fèi　　　　废品 fèipǐn　　　　waste
　　　　　　　废话 fèihuà　　　　nonsense

强	暗	戏	移	量	顺	废

活用园地

Corner for Flexible Usage

一　组词

Form words and phrases.

逗　逗乐儿　amusing　逗笑　funny　逗人　funny
　　逗人喜欢　interesting　逗人发笑　laughter-provoking
　　逗孩子玩儿　tease with children　逗号　comma

露　①lù
　　流露　show unintentionally　显露　reveal
　　露天　in the open(air)
　　不露声色　without betraying what is going on in one's mind
　　②lòu
　　露出　show　露一手　show off one's expertise

缩　缩短　shorten　缩小　reduce　缩减　cut down
　　缩写　abbreviation　紧缩　reduce　压缩　condense
　　收缩　contract

束　一束花　a bunch of flowers　约束　refrain
　　束手束脚　have one's hands and feet tied

速　速成　short and intensified(course,etc.)　速冻　quick-freeze
　　速写　sketch　急速　hurriedly　高速　high speed
　　车速　speed of the vehicle　光速　velocity of light
　　音速　velocity of sound　快速　high-speed　减速　decelerate

剧 电视剧 TV series 喜剧 comedy 剧本 script
剧团 theatrical company 剧院 theatre 急剧 drastically
剧烈 violent

据 收据 receipt 证据 evidence 据点 stronghold

壮 健壮 healthy and strong 壮大 strengthen 壮观 spectacular
壮丽 magnificent 壮烈 heroic 壮志 great aspiration
身强力壮 physically strong

装 装病 pretend to be ill 装傻 pretend to know nothing
服装 clothing 时装 fashion 西装 Western-style suit
军装 military uniform 包装 package 装备 equipment
中山装 Chinese tunic suit

当 当场 on the spot 当前 at present 当心 be careful
当初 at first 当家 manage household affairs 当选 be elected
当中 in the middle 当事人 person concerned
当局 the authorities 当面 in the presence of 应当 should
每当 every time when

挡 挡风 shelter sth. from the wind 挡雨 keep off the rain
挡道 block the way

固 加固 strengthen 牢固 firm 固然 though of course
固有 inherent 固体 solid

占 占有 possess 占领 occupy 占据 occupy
占多数 constitute the majority 占上风 get the upper hand
占便宜 gain extra advantage by unfair means

战 战士 soldier 战斗 battle 战友 comrade-in-arms
战场 battlefield 战胜 conquer 战术 tactics
决战 decisive battle 内战 civil war 停战 cease fire

抱 怀抱 embrace 环抱 surround
抱不平 be outraged by an injustice 抱负 ambition

幻 幻觉 hallucination 幻想曲 fantasia

幼 幼儿 child 幼年 childhood 幼小 young and small

宅 宅子 residence 住宅区 living quarters

闭 闭嘴 shut up 关闭 close 封闭 close
闭门思过 shut oneself up and ponder over one's mistakes

闲 闲话 gossip 闲聊 chit-chat 闲谈 chat

闲不住　refuse to stay idle　闲工夫　leisure

质　本质　nature　实质　essence　品质　quality　物质　matter
气质　disposition　体质　physique　杂质　impurity

压　压缩　compress　压碎　crush　压制　suppress　压扁　flatten
气压　atmospheric pressure　电压　voltage　血压　blood pressure
高血压　hypertension　压岁钱　money given to children as a lunar New Year gift

厌　厌烦　be tired of　厌倦　be tired of　不厌其烦　take great pains
喜新厌旧　love the new and loathe the old——be fickle in one's affections
看厌了　tired of watching　吃厌了　tired of eating
听厌了　tired of hearing

击　打击　attack　反击　counter attack　攻击　attack
回击　beat back　目击　witness　射击　shoot

即　即使　even if　即刻　at once　即日　on the very day
即便　even if　即兴　impromptu　随即　right after

状　现状　status quo　告状　bring a lawsuit against sb.　状语　adverbial

碎　碎片　broken pieces　细碎　in small; broken pieces
零碎　scrappy　破碎　broken

强　强壮　healthy and strong　强烈　strong　强度　strength
强化　strengthen　强制　force

暗　灰暗　gray and dark　昏暗　dim　阴暗　dark　暗示　hint
暗中　secretly　暗地里　stealthily　暗号　signal
暗暗　secretly　暗淡　dim

戏　看戏　go to the theatre　戏院　theatre　戏曲　traditional opera
戏迷　opera fan　京戏　Beijing opera　马戏　circus
演戏　put on a play

移　移民　immigrant　转移　transfer

量　重量　weight　数量　quantity　力量　power; strength
热量　heat　质量　quality　产量　output　雨量　rainfall
降水量　precipitation　音量　volume　酒量　capacity for liquor
少量　a little amount of　商量　talk something over

顺　顺便　incidentally　顺路　on the way
顺风　in the same direction of the wind　顺手　without extra effort
顺耳　pleasing to the ear　顺眼　pleasing to the eye

笔顺　order of strokes　通顺　fluent

废　　废物　waste　废料　waste material　废气　waste gas
　　　废纸　waste paper　废除　abolish　作废　become invalid

二　认读句子

Read and try to understand the following sentences.

1. 我真希望你能在这儿多<u>逗留</u>几天，好好地游览一下<u>当地</u>的名胜古迹。
   I do hope you can stay here longer so that you can visit the scenic spots and historical sites in the locality.

2. 他好久没<u>露面</u>了，也不知道他最近身体<u>状况</u>怎么样。
   He's been obscure for a long time and I wonder how he has been physically in recent days.

3. 比赛已经<u>结束</u>了，可是球迷们还不想走。
   The game was over，but the fans refused to leave.

4. 我刚才叫你，你为什么<u>假装</u>没听见？
   I called you just now.　Why did you pretend not to hear me?

5. <u>据说</u>他小时候就<u>幻想</u>当总统，现在他的愿望终于实现了。
   It's said that he has dreamed of being a president since childhood，and now his dream has come true.

6. 因为我工作很忙，所以我学习汉语没有<u>固定</u>的时间。
   As I am very busy, I do not have fixed time for my Chinese study.

7. 那是小明的姑姑，她是<u>幼儿园</u>的老师。
   That is Xiao Ming's aunt，who is a teacher at a kindergarten.

8. 他身体<u>强壮</u>，跑步的<u>速度</u>很快。
   He is healthy and strong and runs fast.

9. 要和平，不要<u>战争</u>。
   We want no war but peace.

10. 这些东西都是<u>废品</u>，<u>质量</u>太差了。
    These are worthless，and the quality is too poor.

11. 我<u>讨厌</u>拳击，不知道为什么有那么多的人会喜欢这种运动。
    I hate boxing and do not understand why so many people are fond of it.

12. 你一会儿说同意，一会儿说不同意，<u>自相矛盾</u>。
    One moment you say you are for it and at another you say you're against

it. Isn't that self-contradictory?

13. 当我遇到困难的时候，他们给予了我很大帮助。

They gave me a lot of help when I had run into difficulty.

14. 那个公司上个月倒闭了。

That company closed down last month.

15. 我喜欢戏剧，空闲的时候，我经常去那个露天剧场看演出。

I like drama and often go to the open theatre when I have time.

16. 今年，这个城市为教师建造了大量的住宅。

A lot of apartment buildings have been put up for teachers in the city this year.

17. 我心里很矛盾，不知道是继续在中国学习还是回国找工作。

I don't know what to do. Shall I continue my studies in China or go back home to find a job?

18. 他把那几张试卷卷了起来，装进了书包里。

He rolled up the exam papers and put them into the school bag.

19. 真抱歉，我打碎了你的杯子。

I'm very sorry that I've broken your cup.

20. 祝你学习进步，工作顺利。

I wish you progress in your studies and success in your work.

21. 这个箱子放在这儿，挡住了路，你们能不能把它移到那边去？

The box is in the way. Can you move it a bit to that side?

22. 四周一片黑暗，他感到有点儿害怕。

It was dark all around, and he was a little scared.

23. 每个人都希望自己的国家越来越强大。

Everybody hopes that his country is growing more and more powerful.

24. 他最近感到很疲劳，学习的压力很大。

He feels rather tired with the heavy load of his studies.

25. 这种布缩水，所以你应当买大一点儿的。

This kind of cloth shrinks in water. You'd better get one of larger size.

26. 她的菜做得不错，今天让她给你们露一手。

She is a good cook. Let her show off today.

27. 这个电影是根据一个真实的故事改编的。

The film is based on a true story.

28. 朋友有困难，当然要帮助。

It goes without saying that we should extend a helping hand when our friends are in difficulty.

29. 中国的人口<u>占</u>世界人口的五分之一。

China's population takes up one fifth of the world total.

30. 刚才有人来电话，好像有急事，让你<u>立即</u>回家。

There was a phone call just now. It sounded as if there was something urgent and you are wanted to go back home at once.

31. 那个孩子把一<u>束</u>鲜花献给了那位科学家。

The child presented to the scientist a bouquet.

自学园地

Corner for Self-study

一 给下列词语注音

Mark the following words with phonetic symbols.

假装　　　　　　顺　　　　　　强调　　　　　　讨厌　　　　　　立即

(　　　　　)　(　　　　　)　(　　　　　)　(　　　　　)　(　　　　　)

抱歉　　　　　　给予　　　　　　矛盾　　　　　　据说　　　　　　黑暗

(　　　　　)　(　　　　　)　(　　　　　)　(　　　　　)　(　　　　　)

二 组词

Form words and phrases.

速：_____　　_____　　　　据：_____　　_____

状：_____　　_____　　　　当：_____　　_____

质：_____　　_____　　　　强：_____　　_____

剧：_____　　_____　　　　量：_____　　_____

戏：_____　　_____　　　　即：_____　　_____

三 给下列各组汉字注音并组词

Mark the following characters with phonetic symbls, and form words and phrases with them.

须（　　　　）_____ 最（　　　　）_____
顺（　　　　）_____ 量（　　　　）_____

废（　　　　）_____ 古（　　　　）_____
疲（　　　　）_____ 占（　　　　）_____

却（　　　　）_____ 战（　　　　）_____
即（　　　　）_____ 戏（　　　　）_____

四 在括号内填上合适的词语

Fill in the blanks with the right words.

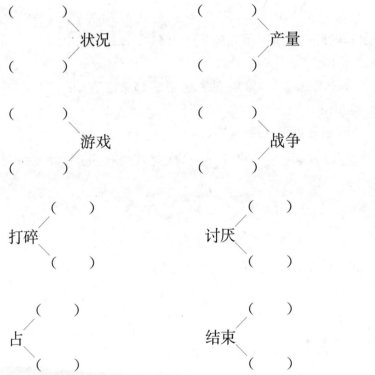

（　　　）
　　　　　状况
（　　　）

（　　　）
　　　　　游戏
（　　　）

（　　　）
打碎
（　　　）

（　　　）
占
（　　　）

（　　　）
　　　　　产量
（　　　）

（　　　）
　　　　　战争
（　　　）

（　　　）
讨厌
（　　　）

（　　　）
结束
（　　　）

（　　　）
　　　　　力量
（　　　）

（　　　）
　　　　　矛盾
（　　　）

（　　　）
战胜
（　　　）

五　阅读下列句子并回答问题

1. 大家要<u>加强</u>团结，不要<u>强调</u>矛盾，团结一心，才有可能提高产品的<u>产量</u>和<u>质量</u>。
   如何提高产量和质量？

2. 大家已经对这支球队不再<u>抱有</u>任何幻想，因为他们的表现太让人失望了，可是谁想到昨天他们的<u>状态</u>特别好，竟然<u>战胜</u>了<u>强大</u>的对手。
   昨天比赛的结果怎么样？

3. <u>据调查</u>，当时他的汽车在<u>高速公路</u>上<u>时速</u>达到了 150 公里，又是长时间疲劳驾驶，事故就这样发生了。
   事故发生的原因是什么？

4. 中国的戏剧中，我比较喜欢<u>京剧</u>，虽然我不太听得懂，但是它的<u>服装</u>、脸谱，我觉得太有意思了。
   说话人为什么喜欢京剧？

5. 现在有些孩子特别喜欢玩儿电子<u>游戏</u>，一玩儿就是好几个小时，作业也不做，学校希望父母跟老师一起，<u>加强</u>对孩子进行这方面的教育。
   学校对家长有什么希望？

6. 最近几年，由于<u>休闲</u>时间的增加，<u>休闲</u>方法也丰富起来了，<u>休闲</u>产业也随之不断地发展<u>壮大</u>起来。
   为什么休闲产业会不断发展壮大？

7. 你说的都是<u>废话</u>，<u>当时</u>的<u>状况</u><u>相当</u>紧急，必须<u>立即</u>作出决定，哪有时间想得那么细？
   "废话"可能是什么？

第十四课

汉字园地
Corner for Chinese Characters

1. 依	yī	depend
依靠	yīkào	depend on
依然	yīrán	still
2. 靠	kào	rely on; lean against
可靠	kěkào	reliable
3. 腰	yāo	waist
腰酸背疼	yāo suān bèi téng	have a sore waist and an aching back
4. 谓	wèi	say
无所谓	wúsuǒwèi	it does not matter
5. 琴	qín	lyre
钢琴	gāngqín	piano
6. 良	liáng	fair
良好	liánghǎo	fair
7. 粮	liáng	grain
粮食	liángshi	grain
8. 材	cái	material
材料	cáiliào	material
教材	jiàocái	teaching material

9. 财	cái	money
财产	cáichǎn	property
发财	fā cái	get rich
10. 狂	kuáng	crazy
狂欢节	Kuánghuān Jié	carnival
11. 逛	guàng	stroll
逛街	guàng jiē	stroll around the streets
12. 描	miáo	depict
描写	miáoxiě	describe
13. 赶	gǎn	catch up with
赶快	gǎnkuài	hurry up
赶上	gǎnshang	catch up with
14. 肝	gān	liver
肝炎	gānyán	hepatitis
15. 杆	gān	pole
旗杆	qígān	flagpole
16. 源	yuán	source
能源	néngyuán	the sources of energy
17. 吐	tǔ	spit
吐气	tǔ qì	breathe out
18. 肚	dù	belly
肚子	dùzi	belly; abdomen; stomach
啤酒肚	píjiǔ dù	beer belly
19. 伯	bó	uncle
伯伯	bóbo	uncle
20. 迫	pò	force
迫切	pòqiè	pressing
21. 归	guī	return
归国	guī guó	return to one's native country

22. 纠	jiū	correct
纠正	jiūzhèng	put right
23. 律	lù	law
律师	lùshī	lawyer
法律	fǎlù	law
规律	guīlù	law；regular pattern
纪律	jìlù	discipline
24. 津	jīn	ford
天津	Tiānjīn	Tianjin
25. 厉	lì	fierce
严厉	yánlì	severe
厉害	lìhai	terrible；formidable
26. 严	yán	strict
严重	yánzhòng	serious
严格	yángé	strict
27. 恶	①è	evil；fierce
恶化	èhuà	worsen
	②wù	dislike
可恶	kěwù	disgusting
28. 曲	qǔ	tune
歌曲	gēqǔ	song
29. 允	yǔn	promise
允许	yǔnxǔ	permit
30. 乒	pīng	
31. 乓	pāng	
乒乓球	pīngpāngqiú	table tennis
32. 坚	jiān	firm
坚持	jiānchí	persevere
坚决	jiānjué	resolute
坚强	jiānqiáng	firm；strong

33. 竖	shù	erect
竖立	shùlì	erect
34. 浪	làng	wave
浪费	làngfèi	waste
35. 狼	láng	wolf
狼狗	lánggǒu	wolfhound
色狼	sèláng	lecher
36. 舅	jiù	mother's brother; maternal uncle
舅舅	jiùjiu	mother's brother
舅妈	jiùmā	wife of mother's brother
37. 鼠	shǔ	mouse
老鼠	lǎoshǔ	rat
鼠标	shǔbiāo	mouse

记忆窍门

Tips for Memorizing Work

一　形声字声旁记忆

Memorize the following characters with the given phonetic elements.

衣　yī

（一）依　depend　依靠　yīkào　　　　rely on
　　　　　　　　依然　yīrán　　　　still

告　gào

（　）告 _____

(kào) 靠　rely on; lean against

　　　　　　　　可靠　kěkào　　　　reliable

（　）造 _____

要　　yāo
　　( )　要　＿＿＿＿＿＿＿＿＿＿＿＿＿
　　(一)　腰　waist　　腰酸背疼　yāo suān bèi téng
　　　　　　　　　　have a sore waist and an aching back

胃　　wèi
　　( )　胃　＿＿＿＿＿＿＿＿＿＿＿＿＿
　　(丶)　谓　say　　无所谓　wúsuǒwèi　　it does not matter

今　　jīn
　　(qín)　琴　lyre　　钢琴　gāngqín　　piano

良　　liáng
　　(ˊ)　良　fair　　良好　liánghǎo　　fair
　　(ˊ)　粮　grain　　粮食　liángshi　　grain

才　　cái
　　( )　材　＿＿＿＿＿＿＿＿＿＿＿＿＿
　　(ˊ)　财　money　　财产　cáichǎn　　property
　　　　　　　　　发财　fā cái　　get rich

狂　　kuáng
　　(ˊ)　狂　crazy　　狂欢节　Kuánghuān Jié　carnival
　　(guàng)　逛　stroll
　　　　　　　　逛街　guàng jiē　stroll around the streets

苗　　miáo
　　( )　苗　＿＿＿＿＿＿＿＿＿＿＿＿＿
　　(ˊ)　描　depict　　描写　miáoxiě　　describe
　　( )　庙　＿＿＿＿＿＿＿＿＿＿＿＿＿
　　( )　猫　＿＿＿＿＿＿＿＿＿＿＿＿＿

干　　gān
　　(ˇ)　赶　catch up with
　　　　　　　赶快　gǎnkuài　　hurry up
　　　　　　　赶上　gǎnshang　　catch up with

（一）肝　liver　　肝炎　gānyán　　　hepatitis
（二）杆　pole　　旗杆　qígān　　　　flagpole
（　）旱　_____

原　yuán

（　）原　_____
（　）愿　_____
（ˊ）源　source　　能源　néngyuán　　source of energy

土　tǔ

（ˋ）吐　spit　　　吐气　tǔ qì　　　　breathe out
（dù）肚　belly　　肚子　dùzi　　　　belly；stomach
　　　　　　　　　啤酒肚　píjiǔ dù　　beer belly

依	靠	腰	谓	琴	良	粮	材	财	狂	逛	描	赶	肝

杆	源	吐	肚

二　比较下列形近字

Compare the following characters with similar pictographic elements.

伯——迫——怕——拍

伯　bó　　uncel　　伯伯　bóbo　　　uncle
迫　pò　　force　　迫切　pòqiè　　　pressing
怕　_____
拍　_____

旧——归

旧　_____
归　guī　　return　　归国　guī guó　　return to one's native country

叫——纠

叫　_____
纠　jiū　　correct　　纠正　jiūzhèng　　　put right

律——津

律	lǜ	law	律师	lǜshī	lawyer
			法律	fǎlǜ	law
			规律	guīlǜ	law
			纪律	jìlǜ	discipline
津	jīn	ford	天津	Tiānjīn	Tianjin

历——厉

历					
厉	lì	fierce	严厉	yánlì	severe
			厉害	lìhài	terrible; formidable

严——恶

严	yán	strict	严重	yánzhòng	serious
			严格	yángé	strict
恶	①è	evil; fierce	恶化	èhuà	worsen
	②wù	dislike	可恶	kěwù	disgusting

由——曲

| 由 | | | | | |
| 曲 | qǔ | tune | 歌曲 | gēqǔ | song |

充——允

| 充 | | | | | |
| 允 | yǔn | promise | 允许 | yǔnxǔ | permit |

乒——乓

| 乒 | pīng | | | | |
| 乓 | pāng | | 乒乓球 | pīngpāngqiú | table tennis |

坚——竖

坚	jiān	firm	坚持	jiānchí	persevere
			坚决	jiānjué	resolute
			坚强	jiānqiáng	firm; strong
竖	shù	erect	竖立	shùlì	erect

浪——狼

| 浪 | làng | wave | 浪费 | làngfèi | waste |

狼	láng	wolf	狼狗	lánggǒu	wolfhound
			色狼	sèláng	lecher

舅——鼠

舅	jiù	mother's brother;uncle			
			舅舅	jiùjiu	mother's brother
			舅妈	jiùmā	wife of mother's brother
鼠	shǔ	mouse	老鼠	lǎoshǔ	rat
			鼠标	shǔbiāo	mouse

伯 迫 归 纠 律 津 厉 严 恶 曲 允 乒 乓 坚

竖 浪 狼 舅 鼠

活用园地
Corner for Flexible Usage

一 组词

Form words and phrases.

依　依照 according to　依据 in accordance with
　　依旧 still　依次 one after another　依然如故 remain the same
　　依依不舍 be reluctant to part

靠　靠得住 reliable　靠不住 unreliable　靠山 backer
　　靠边 keep to the side　靠窗 by the window

响　响声 noise　响亮 loud and clear　音响 acoustics
　　响应 respond to　交响乐 symphony

腰　腰带 belt　腰部 waist　腰身 waist measurement
　　腰疼 lumbago　弯腰 bend down　半山腰 half way up the hill
　　点头哈腰 bow and scrape

谓　所谓 so-called　谓语 predicate

琴 大提琴 cello 小提琴 violin 对牛弹琴 cast pearls before swine

良 良友 good friend 良心 conscience 良机 good opportunity

粮 粮店 grain store 杂粮 food grains other than wheat and rice

粗粮 coarse food grains such as maize, sorghum, millet, etc. as compared with wheat flour and rice

细粮 fine food grains like wheat flour and rice

材 钢材 steel products 木材 timber

药材 medicinal materials 器材 equipment 身材 figure

题材 topic 大材小用 one's talent wasted on a petty job

财 财宝 treasure 财富 fortune 财力 financial capacity

财政 finance 财经 finance and economics

狂 狂妄 arrogant 狂风 violent wind 狂热 zest 狂喜 ecstasy

狂笑 laugh wildly

逛 逛商店 mall hopping 逛大街 stroll around the streets

闲逛 ramble 到处游逛 roam

描 描画 depict 描红 trace in black ink over characters printed in red (in learning to write Chinese characters)

轻描淡写 touch on lightly

猫 小猫 kitty 公猫 tomcat 母猫 female cat 野猫 wild cat

赶 赶紧 hurry 赶忙 in a hurry 赶火车 catch up with the train

赶飞机 catch up with the flight 赶时间 seize the time

赶得上 be able to catch up with 赶不上 be unable to catch up with

肝 肝脏 liver 心肝 darling

源 来源 source 起源 originate 发源 rise

源泉 source 电源 power supply

伯 伯父 uncle 伯母 aunt 大伯 father's eldest brother

老伯 uncle (a polite form used to address elder males)

迫 紧迫 pressing 压迫 oppression 迫害 persecute

被迫 be forced 迫使 force

归 归还 return 总归 after all

纠 纠纷 dispute

律 法律 law 一律 alike

厉 厉害 fierce

严	严重 serious 严密 tight 尊严 dignity 严寒 severe cold
恶	①è
	恶性 malignant 恶果 disastrous effect 恶习 bad habit
	恶作剧 mischief
	②wù
	厌恶 dislike 可恶 disgusting
曲	作曲家 composer 交响曲 symphony 圆舞曲 waltz
	小夜曲 serenade
坚	坚固 solid 坚定 firmly 坚信 firmly believe 坚硬 hard
竖	横七竖八 at sixes and sevens 竖线 vertical line
浪	风浪 stormy waves 海浪 sea waves
	风平浪静 the wind has dropped and the waves have subsided
狼	一只狼 a wolf
	引狼入室 invite a wolf to one's house—open the door to an enemy
	狼狗 wolfhound

二 认读句子

Read and try to understand the following sentences.

1. 他依靠自己的努力,最后取得了成功。
   He succeeded on his own in the end.

2. 昨天我逛了一天的街,逛得腰酸背疼。
   I strolled about the streets all day yesterday and my back ached with fatigue.

3. 他这个人恐怕不太可靠,你不要太相信他。
   Don't trust him as he is not a reliable person.

4. 她从小就学习钢琴。这是受她妈妈的影响,她妈妈是钢琴老师。
   She has learned to play the piano since childhood. That is the result of her mother's influence, who is a piano teacher.

5. 我无所谓,去哪儿玩都可以。
   I don't mind where to go. Any place will do.

6. 小时候,父母常对我说:"不能浪费一粒粮食。"
   When I was a child, my parents often said to me, "You are not to waste a bit of grain."

7. 那套<u>教材</u>,包括语法、汉字、阅读等一共八本。

The set of teaching materials has eight volumes including grammar, Chinese characters and reading.

8. 今天是<u>狂欢节</u>,大街上真热闹。

Today's the carnival and the streets are busy and crowded.

9. 那篇小说<u>描写</u>了最近几年中国农村农民生活的情况。

That story gives a description of Chinese peasants' life in the country in recent years.

10. 要下雨了,<u>赶快</u>走吧。

It threatens to rain. Let's hurry.

11. 王师傅是<u>天津人</u>。

Master Wang is from Tianjin.

12. 他<u>伯伯</u>是一名<u>归国</u>华侨。

His uncle is a returned overseas Chinese.

13. 我<u>迫切</u>需要一个辅导老师来帮助我<u>纠正</u>发音。

I need badly a tutor who can help correct my pronunciation.

14. 他父母对他很<u>严格</u>,从小就要求他养成<u>良好</u>的习惯。

His parents have been strict with him since his childhood. They want him to form a good habit.

15. 世界人口越来越多,<u>能源</u>越来越缺乏。

While the world population is growing, the sources of energy are dwindling.

16. 他会唱很多中国<u>歌曲</u>。

He can sing a lot of Chinese songs.

17. <u>旗杆</u>就<u>竖</u>在这儿吧。

Let's erect the flagpole here.

18. 他家养了一只猫,还养了一只大<u>狼狗</u>。

They raise a cat and a big wolfhound.

19. 领导<u>允许</u>他请一个星期假,回家看看父母。

The leader gave him a week's leave to go home to see his parents.

20. 我每天<u>坚持</u>打一个小时<u>乒乓</u>球。

I keep playing table tennis for an hour every day.

21. 我爸爸是一个律师,他是一个很<u>严厉</u>的人,我从小就对他很害怕。

My father is a lawyer. He is a very serious person and I have been afraid of him since my childhood.

22. 他妈妈得了<u>肝炎</u>,他们家却没有钱让她住院看病。

His mother got hepatitis, but his family was too poor to send her to hospital.

23. 国旗在<u>旗杆</u>上慢慢上升。
The national flag is rising slowly on the flagpole.

24. 他这个人很<u>狂</u>，总是觉得自己比别人强。
He's rather arrogant and always thinks that he's better off than others.

25. 这些<u>财产</u>都是他爷爷留下来的。
All the property was left over by his grandfather.

26. 知识就是<u>财富</u>。
Knowledge is wealth.

27. 师傅，我要赶飞机，你能不能把车开快点儿？我快<u>赶不上</u>了。
Master, I'm going to catch a flight. Can't you drive a little faster? There's little time left.

28. 今天刮风，湖里<u>浪</u>很大，不能划船了。
It's windy today, and the waves are very high. so we cannot go boating on the lake.

29. 你们俩<u>靠近</u>一点儿，我给你们照一张相。
Stand closer, you two. I'll take a photo for you.

30. 我爸爸是个<u>律师</u>，每天总是一副很<u>严厉</u>的样子，我跟他很少交流。
My father is a lawyer, and he is always putting on a stern look. I have little communication with him.

自学园地
Corner for Self-study

一　给下列词语注音
Mark the following words and phrases with phonetic symbols

材料　　坚强　　赶快　　钢琴　　歌曲
(　　) (　　) (　　) (　　) (　　)

浪费　　允许　　能源　　律师　　无所谓
(　　) (　　) (　　) (　　) (　　)

二 写出本课含有下列偏旁的汉字并注音

Write out the characters with the following elements in this lesson, and mark them with phonetic symbols.

氵：_____（　　　）　　_____（　　　）　　_____（　　　）

月：_____（　　　）　　_____（　　　）　　_____（　　　）

木：_____（　　　）　　_____（　　　）

亻：_____（　　　）　　_____（　　　）

辶：_____（　　　）　　_____（　　　）

犭：_____（　　　）　　_____（　　　）

三 组词

Form words and phrases.

材：_____　_____　　　　赶：_____　_____

琴：_____　_____　　　　恶：_____　_____

坚：_____　_____　　　　严：_____　_____

律：_____　_____　　　　依：_____　_____

逛：_____　_____　　　　财：_____　_____

四 根据意思把左右两栏用线连起来

Link the word in the left column with the one in the right column that matches it in meaning.

坚决的	后果		依靠	景色
严格的	心情		挑选	时间
迫切的	决心		描写	父母
丰富的	制度		坚持	牌子
坚强的	态度		竖立	材料
严重的	材料		浪费	意见

五　阅读下列句子并回答问题

Read the following sentences and answer the questions accordingly.

1. 老人的病突然开始<u>恶化</u>，病情越来越<u>严重</u>，他在国外工作的儿子昨天也<u>赶</u>了回来。

   老人的儿子为什么从国外回来了？

2. 我看，我们无论怎么劝，她也不会改变想法的，她的态度<u>依然</u>是那么<u>坚决</u>。

   "我们"的劝告有没有用？

3. 这本教材把汉语的语法规律介绍得很清楚，我在国内学习语法时就是靠这本书，它帮了我很大的忙。

   "我"在国内是怎么学习汉语语法的？

4. 你每天都在做<u>发财</u>梦，但是任何成功都要<u>依靠</u>自己的努力才能得到，像你这样，每天什么都不想干，怎么可能发财？

   "你"每天在想什么？

5. "d、t、p"这几个音，我总是发不好，为了纠正我的发音，老师让我不断地练习这样的句子："吃葡萄不<u>吐</u>葡萄皮儿，不吃葡萄倒<u>吐</u>葡萄皮儿。"

   老师为什么让"我"不断练习那个句子？

6. 他有胃病，刚才<u>肚子</u>疼得<u>厉害</u>，还把吃的东西都吐出来了。

   他怎么了？

7. <u>舅舅</u>是从德国留学回来，他们这样的人习惯上被人们叫做"<u>海归派</u>"，意思是从海外留学回来的，<u>舅舅</u>出国前还很瘦，可在德国五年后回来，却胖得我快认不出来了，<u>舅妈</u>说，<u>舅舅</u>的<u>啤酒肚</u>是喝啤酒喝出来的，因为德国人爱喝啤酒，德国的啤酒世界有名。

   出国前后，舅舅为什么变化？

8. 因为<u>鼠标</u>的样子有点像<u>老鼠</u>，所以才被叫做"<u>鼠标</u>"。我怎么没看出来它像<u>老鼠</u>？

   为什么把它叫做鼠标？

第十五课

汉字园地
Corner for Chinese Characters

1. 励	lì	encourage
鼓励	gǔlì	encourage
2. 斗	dòu	strife
斗争	dòuzhēng	struggle
3. 抖	dǒu	shake
发抖	fādǒu	tremble
4. 君	jūn	monarch
君主制	jūnzhǔzhì	monarchy
5. 群	qún	crowd; group
群众	qúnzhòng	the masses
6. 率	①shuài	lead
率领	shuàilǐng	lead
	②lù	rate; proportion
效率	xiàolù	efficiency
7. 摔	shuāi	fall
摔倒	shuāidǎo	tumble
8. 代	dài	take the place of; generation
代表	dàibiǎo	representative
现代	xiàndài	modern times
现代化	xiàndàihuà	modernize
时代	shídài	times
年代	niándài	age

9. 袋	dài	bag
脑袋	nǎodai	head
口袋	kǒudai	bag
10. 粉	fěn	powder
粉笔	fěnbǐ	chalk
粉红色	fěnhóngsè	pink
11. 纷	fēn	many and various
纷纷	fēnfēn	in profusion; one after another
12. 份	fèn	copy
一份报纸	yí fèn bàozhǐ	a (copy of) newspaper
身份证	shēnfènzhèng	identity card
备份	bèifèn	backup
13. 并	bìng	and
并且	bìngqiě	also
14. 饼	bǐng	pie
饼干	bǐnggān	biscuit
15. 拼	pīn	spell; join together
拼音	pīnyīn	spell
拼命	pīn mìng	desperately
16. 粘	zhān	glue
粘住	zhānzhù	stick to
17. 钻	①zuān	drill
钻研	zuānyán	study intensively
	②zuàn	diamond
钻石	zuànshí	diamond
18. 勾	gōu	induce; tick off
勾起	gōuqǐ	evoke
19. 购	gòu	purchase
购买	gòumǎi	buy
20. 构	gòu	construct
结构	jiégòu	structure
构成	gòuchéng	form
构想	gòuxiǎng	concept

21.	尚	shàng	esteem
	时尚	shíshàng	fashion
22.	党	dǎng	party
	政党	zhèngdǎng	political party
23.	私	sī	private
	私人	sīrén	private
24.	否	fǒu	negate
	否定	fǒudìng	negate
	是否	shìfǒu	whether or not
	否则	fǒuzé	otherwise
25.	弱	ruò	weak
	软弱	ruǎnruò	weak
26.	存	cún	deposit
	存在	cúnzài	exist
	保存	bǎocún	preserve
27.	浓	nóng	thick
	浓茶	nóng chá	strong tea
28.	淡	dàn	thin; tasteless
	冷淡	lěngdàn	cold
29.	繁	fán	in great numbers
	繁荣	fánróng	prosperous
	繁华	fánhuá	flourishing
30.	优	yōu	superior
	优点	yōudiǎn	merit
	优良	yōuliáng	good
	优美	yōuměi	graceful
31.	劣	liè	inferior
	劣质	lièzhì	of inferior quality
32.	款	kuǎn	a sum of money
	存款	cún kuǎn	deposit money (in a bank)
	大款	dàkuǎn	moneybags

33. 疑	yí	doubt
怀疑	huáiyí	doubt
疑问	yíwèn	qestion
无疑	wúyí	undoubtedly
34. 启	qǐ	open
启发	qǐfā	inspire
启动	qǐdòng	start; switch on
35. 卫	wèi	safeguard
卫生	wèishēng	hygiene
卫星	wèixīng	satellite
保卫	bǎowèi	defend
36. 丽	lì	beauty
美丽	měilì	beautiful
37. 鼓	gǔ	drum
鼓掌	gǔzhǎng	applaud
鼓舞	gǔwǔ	inspire; inspiration

记忆窍门

Tips for Memorizing Work

一　形声字声旁记忆

Memorize the following characters with the given phonetic elements.

厉　lì

（　）厉 _____

（丶）励　encourage　　　鼓励　gǔlì　　　　encourage

斗　dòu

（丶）斗　strife　　　斗争　dòuzhēng　　　struggle

（　）抖　shake　　　发抖　fādǒu　　　shiver

君　jūn

（一）君　monarch　　　君主制　jūnzhǔzhì　　monarchy

（　）裙 _____

（qún）群　crowd;group　群众　qúnzhòng　　the masses

率　shuài

（丶）率　lead　　　　率领　shuàilǐng　　lead

（lǜ）率　rate;proportion　效率　xiàolǜ　　efficiency

（一）摔　fall　　　　摔倒　shuāidǎo　　tumble

代　dài

（丶）代　take the place of; generation

代表　dàibiǎo　　represent

现代　xiàndài　　modern times

现代化　xiàndàihuà　modernize

时代　shídài　　times

年代　niándài　　age

（丶）袋　bag　　　脑袋　nǎodai　　head

口袋　kǒudai　　bag

分　fēn

（ˇ）粉　powder　　粉笔　fěnbǐ　　chalk

粉红色　fěnhóngsè　pink

（一）纷　many and various

纷纷　fēnfēn　　one after another

（丶）份　copy　　　一份报纸　yí fèn bàozhǐ　a newspaper

身份证　shēnfènzhèng　identity card

备份　bèifèn　　backup

并　bìng

（丶）并　and　　　并且　bìngqiě　　also

（ˇ）饼　pie　　　饼干　bǐnggān　　biscuit

（pīn）拼　spell;join together

拼音　pīnyīn　　spell

拼命　pīn mìng　　desperately

占　zhàn

（　）站 _____

（　）战 _____

（ˉ）粘　glue　　　　粘住　zhānzhù　　　stick to

（zuān）钻　drill　　　钻研　zuānyán　　　study intensively

（zuàn）钻　jewel　　钻石　zuànshí　　　diamond

勾　gōu

（ˉ）勾　induce; tick of　勾起　gōuqǐ　　　evoke

（ˋ）购　purchase　　　购买　gòumǎi　　　buy

（ˋ）构　construct　　　结构　jiégòu　　　structure

构成　gòuchéng　　form

构想　gòuxiǎng　　concept

尚　shàng

（　）常 _____

（　）掌 _____

（ˋ）尚　esteem　　　时尚　shíshàng　　fashion

（　）堂 _____

（dǎng）党　party　　政党　zhèngdǎng　political party

励 斗 抖 君 群 率 摔 代 袋 粉 纷 份 并 饼

拼 粘 钻 勾 购 构 尚 党

二　比较下列反义词

Compare the following antonyms.

公——私

公 _____

私　sī　private　　　私人　sīrén　　private

是——否

是					
否	fǒu	negate	否定	fǒudìng	negate
			是否	shìfǒu	whether or not
			否则	fǒuzé	otherwise

强——弱

强					
弱	ruò	weak	软弱	ruǎnruò	weak

存——取

存	cún	deposit	存在	cúnzài	exist
			保存	bǎocún	preserve
取					

浓——淡

浓	nóng	thick	浓茶	nóng chá	strong tea
淡	dàn	thin; tasteless	冷淡	lěngdàn	cold

繁——简

繁	fán	numerous	繁荣	fánróng	prosperous
			繁华	fánhuá	flourishing
简					

优——劣

优	yōu	superior	优点	yōudiǎn	merit
			优良	yōuliáng	good
			优美	yōuměi	graceful
劣	liè	inferior	劣质	lièzhì	of inferior quality

私	否	弱	存	浓	淡	繁	优	劣

三 用字组词

Memorize the following words formed by the given characters.

款	kuǎn	存款	cúnkuǎn	deposit money
		大款	dàkuǎn	moneybags man
疑	yí	怀疑	huáiyí	doubt
		疑问	yíwèn	question
		无疑	wúyí	undoubtedly
启	qǐ	启发	qǐfā	inspire
		启动	qǐdòng	start; switch on
卫	wèi	卫生	wèishēng	hygiene
		卫星	wèixīng	satellite
		保卫	bǎowèi	defend
丽	lì	美丽	měilì	beautiful
鼓	gǔ	鼓掌	gǔ zhǎng	applaud
		鼓舞	gǔwǔ	inspire; inspirafion

款	疑	启	卫	丽	鼓

活用园地

Corner for Flexible Usage

一 组词

Form words and phrases.

励	激励 encourage
斗	战斗 fight 决斗 duel
抖	冷得发抖 shiver with cold 抖动 shake
	抖一抖身上的雪 shake off the snow from one's body

君	君子 gentleman	君主 monarch	国君 monarch
群	人群 crowds of people	羊群 herds of sheep	群体 group
	一群人 a group of people	害群之马 an evil member of the herd	

率
①shuài
坦率 frank　草率 sloppy　轻率 reckless　率先 take the lead
②lǜ
比率 ratio　利率 interest rate　概率 probability
生产率 productivity　出生率 birth rate　死亡率 death rate

摔　摔跟头 tumble　摔跤 wrestling

代　代表团 delegation　代词 pronoun
代办 do something for another person
古代 ancient times　近代 modern times
当代 the contemporary era　世代 generation after generation

袋　袋子 bag　脑袋 head　麻袋 gunnybag
热水袋 hot-water bag

粉　粉碎 break into pieces　粉末 powder　面粉 flour
奶粉 milk powder

纷　纷乱 chaotic　大雪纷飞 snow falling in profusion

份　年份 year　月份 month　股份 stock　一份礼品 a present

并　并列 side by side　并排 side by side　合并 merge

饼　月饼 moon cake　烧饼 sesame seed cake
油饼 deep-fried dough cake　比萨饼 pizza

拼　拼写 spelling

勾　勾出来 draw an outline　勾结 hand in glove

购　采购 purchase　订购 order　选购 select and buy
邮购 mail-order　收购 buy　购并 buy and merger

构　构造 structure　构图 composition　构建 compose
构思 work out the plot of a story or composition of a painting
构想 idea　构词法 word-formation　机构 organization

尚　高尚 noble　风尚 prevailing custom　尚且 even
和尚 monk　礼尚往来 courtesy demands reciprocity

党　党员 party member　入党 join the Party
共产党 the Communist Party　党中央 the Party Central Committee
党派 political parties and groups　党性 Party spirit

私　私有　privately owned　私有制　private ownership
　　私自　privately　私营　privately run　私立学校　private school
　　私生活　private life　私生子　illegitimate child　私下　in private
　　自私　selfish　自私自利　selfish

否　否认　refuse to admit　否决　veto　是否　whether or not

弱　弱点　weak point　弱小　small and weak　弱者　the weak
　　减弱　weaken　年老体弱　old and weak

存　存放　deposit　存款　deposit money　生存　exist
　　存车处　bicycle parking lot

浓　浓度　density　浓缩　condensed　浓厚　dense

淡　淡水　fresh water　淡季　off season

繁　繁忙　busy　繁重　heavy　繁多　numerous
　　繁体字　the original complex form of a simplified Chinese character

优　优越　superior　优先　priority　优质　of high quality
　　优胜　superior　优异　excellent

劣　恶劣　bad　低劣　inferior　劣质　of inferior quality

款　款式　style　借款　borrow money　赔款　pay an indemnity
　　欠款　owe a debt　条款　article　公款　public fund
　　付款　payment　款待　entertain

疑　疑问　doubt　疑心　suspecion　可疑　doubtful
　　疑难　knotty　疑难问题　a knotty problem
　　半信半疑　half-believing　坚信不疑　firmly believe

启　启示　revelation　启事　notice　启程　set out　启动　start

卫　卫星　satellite　自卫　self-defence
　　门卫　entrance guard　保卫　defend

丽　华丽　resplendent　壮丽　magnificent
　　风和日丽　a bright sun and a gentle breeze

鼓　鼓动　agitate　鼓吹　advocate　打鼓　beat the drum
　　打退堂鼓　beat a retreat

二 认读句子

Read and try to understand the following sentences.

1. 爸爸常常鼓励我，要与自己的病痛做斗争。
   My father often encourages me to fight against my illness.

2. 他们国家是一个君主制的国家。
   Their country is a monarchy.

3. 哪个答案是对的，请你把它勾出来。
   Please tick the correct answers.

4. 南京路是上海最繁华的街道，街道两侧有很多大的商店。
   The busiest street in Shanghai is Nanjing Road，along which are lined with big department stores and shops.

5. 这里环境优美，空气新鲜，真是一个美丽的地方。
   With fresh air and beautiful scenery，it is a wonderful place.

6. 现在，减肥好像是一种时尚，特别是年轻的姑娘，都想让自己瘦一点儿，再瘦一点儿。
   Nowadays it seems to be a fashion to go on a diet，especially among young girls，who are eager to lose weight to look thinner and thinner.

7. 我想贷款(dài kuǎn)购买一辆汽车。
   I would like to buy a car on credit.

8. 拼音文字和汉语有很大的不同。
   Alphabetic writing languages differ greatly from the Chinese language.

9. 由董事长率领的贸易代表团今天来中国访问。
   A trade delegation led by the chairman of the board is coming to China for a visit today.

10. 他取得了比赛第一名，大家纷纷为他鼓掌。
    He won the first place and all applauded for his success.

11. 我父母总是怀疑我的能力，觉得我这也不行，那也不行。
    My parents have always had little confidence in me，thinking I am good for nothing.

12. 这份《中国日报》，麻烦你好好保存。
    Can I bother you to preserve this copy of *China Daily*?

13. 每个政党都要依靠群众，才能把工作做好。
    Only by relying on the masses can any political party do a good job.

14. 这些都是<u>劣质</u><u>粉笔</u>,不好用。

These pieces of chalk do not write well because they are of inferior quality.

15. 初级听力材料一定要<u>结构</u>简单,<u>否则</u>就可能听不懂。

There should not be complicated structures in elementary listening material, otherwise it may be too difficult to understand.

16. 今天怎么这么冷? 我都冷得<u>发抖</u>了。

How come it is so cold today? I'm shivering with cold.

17. 她以前的男朋友性格太<u>软弱</u>,并<u>且</u>也很<u>自私</u>,所以她跟他分手了。

She left her former boy friend for his weak character and selfishness.

18. 在老师的<u>启发</u>下,他终于掌握了这个语法。

He finally grasped the grammar point with the teacher's elicitation.

19. 那个孩子<u>摔倒</u>了,他妈妈却不去扶他,要他自己爬起来。

The boy had a fall, and instead of helping him up, his mother encouraged him to stand up on his own.

20. 你饿不饿? 我这儿还有点儿<u>饼干</u>。

Are you hungry? I have got some biscuits.

21. 我睡觉前不能喝<u>浓茶</u>,<u>否则</u>睡不着觉。

I cannot drink strong tea before going to bed. Otherwise, I cannot fall asleep.

22. 那边有一个<u>存</u>车处,我们的车就放那边去吧。

There's a bicycle parking lot over there. Let's park our bikes there.

23. 他跟他们领导<u>私人</u>关系不错。

He has a close personal relations with his leaders.

24. 那个姑娘唱完以后,大家都为她<u>鼓掌</u>。

Everybody applauded for her when the girl had finished her songs.

25. <u>大款</u>就是很有钱的人。

A moneybag is a person who has a lot of money.

26. 这本书的最后几页都<u>粘</u>在一起了,麻烦你给我换一本吧。

Please change this book for another one. You see the last few pages are stuck together.

自学园地

Corner for Self-study

一　给下列词语注音

Mark the following words and phrases with phonetic symbols.

优点　　　　怀疑　　　　鼓舞　　　　美丽　　　　购买
(　　　　　)　(　　　　　)　(　　　　　)　(　　　　　)　(　　　　　)

保存　　　　冷淡　　　　代表团　　　现代化　　　身份证
(　　　　　)　(　　　　　)　(　　　　　)　(　　　　　)　(　　　　　)

二　写出本课含有下列偏旁的汉字并注音

Write out the characters with the following elements in this lesson, and mark them with phonetic symbols.

分：_____ (　　　　) _____ (　　　　) _____ (　　　　)

食：_____ (　　　　) _____ (　　　　) _____ (　　　　)

代：_____ (　　　　) _____ (　　　　) _____ (　　　　)

勹：_____ (　　　　) _____ (　　　　) _____ (　　　　)

占：_____ (　　　　) _____ (　　　　) _____ (　　　　)

并：_____ (　　　　) _____ (　　　　) _____ (　　　　)

三　写出反义词

Give the antonym to each of the following words.

强_____　　　　遵守_____

是_____　　　　减少_____

迟_____　　　　节省_____

优_____　　　　聪明_____

简_____　　　　整齐_____

淡_____　　　　表扬_____

硬_____		睁眼_____	
取_____		胆小_____	
公_____		反对_____	
输_____		放大_____	
同_____		冷淡_____	
明_____		软弱_____	
贵_____		肯定_____	
横_____		复杂_____	

四 **根据意思把左右两栏用线连起来**

Link the word in the left column with the one in the right column that matches it in meaning.

态度	优良	积极	怀疑
风景	复杂	纷纷	启发
经济	软弱	刻苦	报导
成绩	优美	大胆	钻研
性格	冷淡	热情	斗争
结构	繁荣	坚决	鼓励

五 **阅读下列句子并回答问题**

Read the following sentences and answer the questions accordingly.

1. 一个人不能只看到自己的<u>优点</u>，而看不到自己的缺点。<u>是否</u>能不断地发扬<u>优点</u>，克服缺点，这是一个人能<u>否</u>不断进步的关键。

   一个人怎么样才能不断进步？

2. 20世纪40<u>年代</u>到60<u>年代</u>，世界上曾经<u>战争</u>不断，而现在，虽然<u>时代</u>不同了，但战争的危险依然<u>存在</u>。

   现在是否还存在战争的可能性？

3. 这个孩子<u>脑袋</u>特别聪明，好像没花什么力气就考上了重点大学，而我的孩子，每天都在<u>拼命</u>学习，结果却还是让人失望。

   这两个孩子有什么不同？

4. 这本书介绍了新的语法体系的构成。它的优点是结构清楚，但是在一些方面，我也存在着一些疑问，不能完全同意作者的意见。

   "我"觉得这本书怎么样？

5. 国家领导人关于经济工作的讲话鼓舞了广大的群众，使他们对今后经济的繁荣发展充满了信心。

   领导人的讲话起到了什么作用？

6. 小卫，困了就睡，在疲劳状态下学习脑袋都发昏，学习效率一定不高。

   小卫怎么啦？

7. 我们对体育馆的设计只是刚刚有了一个初步的构想，真正的设计工作还没有正式启动。

   体育馆的设计进行得怎么样？

8. 你应该先把电脑中的文件备份、保存到软盘或光盘，这样才能防止文件的丢失或其他意外情况的发生。

   怎样防止电脑中的文件丢失？

后　记

　　本书的编写最早始于 1998 年。2000 年,在英国牛津大学召开的"以英语为母语者的汉语教学研讨会"上,作者曾就"汉字教学规律"及本书的编写思路与与会的海内外学者进行过交流。从 2000 年开始,在我所任教的北京语言大学,本书曾分别作为汉字必修课和选修课教材在学院内使用。

　　我从事对外汉语教学工作近十八年,其间大部分的教学对象是零起点的来华留学生。在整个对外汉语教学体系中,汉字教学显示出相对落后的局面,成为对外汉语教学中难以突破的瓶颈。本人在多年的教学实践中也发现,在对外汉字教学这一问题上,我们自觉或不自觉地存在着以下误区:

　　1. 关于汉字教学的定位:从某种程度上说,我们常常只是把汉字作为一种学习的工具,一种记录口语的工具,而忽略了汉字作为书面交际工具的作用。其实,日常语言交际内容不只是以口头形式出现,有的往往是以书面形式呈现的,如:标识、招牌等,只学拼音,不学汉字,也会影响到日常的交际。

　　2. 关于"语"和"文"的关系:以往,我们对此的争论更多集中在语文分开、语文同步、抑或语文分步进行等问题上。在这一点上,可能更重要的还不在于如何处理"语"和"文"的关系,而是如何对待"文",即如何对待汉字的认读与书写。我们认为,初级阶段汉字的认读和书写需要适当分流,从而减轻学生的负担。比如:零起点精读课生词只要求认读,不要求书写,加强语音和口语交际能力方面的训练。独立的汉字课则可以根据汉字自身规律输入汉字,由易到难,并自始至终注意在词语境和句语境中复现。另外,汉字课的汉字应尽快向精读课的生字和生词靠拢,两种课型的词汇逐渐重合,其中的交叉词汇可以为另一课型的词汇学习提供方便。

　　3. 关于汉字教学的阶段:在目前的教学实践中,汉字教学常常只体现为写字教学,即体现在汉字的笔顺、笔画、书写规则等的教学上。其实,汉字教学是一项长期的教学任务,它应该贯穿于汉语教学的始终。初级阶段汉字教学的任务更重要的体现在如何将汉字学习内容与学生的学习策略整合,并根据汉字的构字规律将汉字归纳分类,成群分级呈现,使之互为联想和类推的依靠。汉字学习,从某种意义上说,应该是一种方法和习惯的养成。

　　4. 关于汉字教学的对象:教学对象上的一刀切,也是目前汉字教学中普遍存在的问题。汉字教学不但要考虑到汉字圈和非汉字圈学习者的不同,还要考虑到本科与进修、长期与短期学生不同的学习目的。有些汉语进修生，学习时间只有半年，如果把大量的时间化在学习汉字的书写上，客观上就会影响到他们听说能力的提高，也会造成他们对汉语的畏难情绪，从而使他们失去学习的兴趣和信心。

鉴于以上分析，如果编写独立的汉字教材，开设独立的汉字课程，汉字教学的认读和书写就可适当分流，也可以针对不同的教学对象、不同的教学阶段完成不同的汉字教学任务。汉字课如果作为选修课，则可供日韩等汉字圈学生及不愿意学习汉字书写的非汉字圈学生自由选择，从而满足学生个性化的需求。

《张老师教汉字》从构思、编写、试用到付梓成书，历经数年，因受教学模式、教学观念以及其他一些因素的影响，使我产生了不少的困扰，其间几易其稿，是在出版社的大力支持及编辑们的坚持和督促下，才有机会和大家见面。在此，要衷心感谢北京语言大学出版社所有参与本书编辑出版的老师，还要感谢所有给我提供过帮助和支持的人们！

《张老师教汉字》的《汉字识写课本》及练习册的英译为熊文华老师，插图为丁永寿老师，《汉字拼读课本》的英译为沈叙伦老师，他们的参与为本书增色许多，在此一并致谢！

张惠芬